Help! I'm Raising My Kids While Doing Ministry

Raising Great Kids While Doing Great Ministry

Josh Mayo

xulon PRESS

Contents

Foreword:
Jeanne Mayo (mom)

It's been 27 years since I held my firstborn son in my arms right after he made his appearance into the world. I remember softly whispering to him, "Josh, you and your mom are going to be great friends." How profoundly accurate those words have proven to be.

And now, 27 years later, I find myself writing a forward to his book on raising kids while doing ministry. I stop to almost pinch myself. How could any mom be so fortunate?

Just please be sure of one thing. Sam and Jeanne Mayo (Josh's parents) do not set themselves up as resident experts in this challenging arena called "parenting." But both of our sons have been repeatedly asked, "How did your parents do fulltime ministry and still have both of their children came out 'normal' and Christ-honoring?" So, Josh quietly began to chronicle part of the journey of his growing up years in the Mayo household. You now hold in your hands the end product of that reflection and writing.

The journey of raising our sons while both doing fulltime ministry has not been without mishap or challenge. I remember crying myself to sleep on more than one occasion, drained beyond measure in my attempts to "keep all the balls in the air." But I had made one silent and irrevocable determination that was my "north star" throughout the whole run: *my family was going to always come before my ministry.* You see, my definition of personal success is having "those who know me best, love me most." I realized that youth ministries, churches, and national speaking platforms were going to come and go. But the deposit I put into my sons was going to be the one thing that would emphatically follow me to the very end. To me, it was not so much a matter of deciding *between* my two sons and the ministry. Instead, I truly believed that "the Mayo boys" *were* my ministry.

At the time of this writing, I have been in fulltime youth ministry for nearly four decades. The mood of the church world has seen some pretty big paradigm shifts during those years. When I first began the journey of Christian motherhood, the "submission craze" was peaking. Christian women were often made to feel that if they did anything outside of their home work-wise that their priorities were Scripturally incorrect and deeply sinful. So for the first 10 or so years of Josh's life, I was hounded by critics who crescendoed that my sons would inevitably walk away from Christ because I was not a "stay-at-home-mom." The guilt and self-doubt I sometimes had to claw through was agonizing at best. No one seemed to believe that you could be aggressively involved in ministry while still managing to keep your family your first priority. By God's grace, I quietly determined to prove them wrong.

Many years later, there now seems to be a new twist to the ministry couples I see emerging in the church world. It often seems now that though "dad" is involved in ministry, "mom" quietly removes herself from most every level of involvement except Sunday morning church attendance. Males whose wives are nowhere to be found often lead church ministries in most every arena.

Thus, I often struggle to find many females who are in ANY church ministry trench at all after their first child appears on the scene. The disappearance of these moms not only leaves many young girls without a female role model, but also leaves the emerging generation wondering what a Christian mom really looks like. Granted, the mom's disappearance is done quite nobly in the name of "family." But the long haul consequences of this void may be more serious than we have allowed ourselves to realize.

Please know that I'm not lobbying for moms to have anything close to "fulltime involvement" in church ministries. I'm just concerned that after children enter the scene, many women seem to do a total disappearing act from all forms of church ministry. I really want to lovingly challenge this dangerous pattern. I think it is both possible and fulfilling for Christian moms to have *some limited role* in church-related ministry while also raising their families. This might be something as simple as having coffee once a week with a couple of young girls in the youth group or the continued availability for the people to whom you feel called to minister. I realize that this approach takes both effort and determination. But the long haul spiritual fruit would be significant. Moreover, children would grow up seeing their parents model spiritual commitment and balance on a daily basis.

Granted, this balancing act for Christian parents is not an easy one. But Josh's words will help to chronicle a few of the principles and pragmatics that helped to anchor our run at this strategic goal. And smilingly, I can tell you today that they worked. Both of our amazing sons, Josh and Justin, love the Lord with all their hearts and are involved in fulltime Christian service. And equally rewarding, both of them deeply love their mom and dad. How could life get much better?

If you ever visit our home in Atlanta, you will see a large, framed document that takes center-stage over our stairwell in our home's entrance. It's entitled "The Mayo Family Creed." Those twelve carefully crafted beliefs have helped to anchor all of us through the breathtakingly exciting times in ministry and through some of the agonizing "train wrecks" along the way. But as we reminded ourselves in the 11th statement in our creed: *"Though most of our friends will come and go, I will remain deeply committed to our family. The Mayo Family stands as my 'God-given anchor' and the 'cheering squad' that is always in my corner."*

All I know is that though the Lord has allowed me to speak before massive crowds in His name and experience an undeserved measure of what some would call "ministry success," all of that pales in comparison to the fulfillment of being Josh and Justin Mayo's mom. I have been privileged to make the all-important journey of parenthood with the greatest man I have ever known, their father. And together, we have chosen daily to conduct the balancing act of whole-hearted ministry involvement while being whole-hearted Christian parents.

The result? Well, I really am one of the most blessed, fulfilled women in the world. After all, how many moms get to write a forward for their son's book on how he was parented? I have spent my life challenging youth ministers around the globe to be "Jesus with skin on." I can only thank the Lord that I have been able to be that to my own cherished family along the journey. Yes, critics shook their heads at me when I declined large speaking engagements so I wouldn't have to miss my sons' soccer games. But I knew then...and still believe now...that many people could speak at state youth conventions. *But only one woman in the world could be Josh and Justin's mom.*

The secret to the whole thing? Sam and Jeanne Mayo have just consistently focused on being "people of Christ's love." And around that framework, whether in the church or at home, everything has fallen into place. Let me close by sharing one of my favorite quotes:

"Someday, after we have mastered the winds and the waves, the tides and gravity, we will harness the energy and power of God's love. And then for the second time in the history of mankind, the world will have discovered fire."

I am eternally grateful that because of God's grace and my family, I have re-discovered fire. Lovingly Honored to be "Josh and Justin's Mom,"

Jeanne Mayo
Youth Communicator and
President, Youth Leaders' Coach

P.S. It may surprise you that though I have read segments of Josh's book, I have chosen not to read it yet in total before it goes to print. Why? Because though Sam and Jeanne Mayo were far from perfect parents, I knew that these pages would contain nothing I would secretly desire to edit.

So maybe that's a great goal for all Christian parents: Live your life in such a fashion that if one of your children should decide to write a book about your family, you could enthusiastically say, "Go for it! And give me the first signed copy when it comes out."

Acknowledgments:

Mom and Dad – Sam and Jeanne Mayo
Without you this book wouldn't be possible…literally. I love you both
so much. Thank you so much for not only showing me how to be
successful in ministry, but how to be hugely successful in the most important area – our family. Words cannot express my love and gratitude!
I.L.Y.M.T.L.M.W.A.B.T.C.

Monica Mayo
To my beautiful wife – I adore you. Thanks for believing in me! I am so
excited about what our future holds and the God-given opportunity for us
to live out the principles found in the following pages. You are the reason
why I believe we're going to be "ok at all of this."

Justin Mayo
Hey bro! This crazy book is finally done! Thanks for being the best P.R./
Marketing Agent, not to mention brother, I could ever have. I would be
lost without you. I'm so thankful for all the memories that we have shared
as a family and as brothers. I know there are still a lot more to come.
Love you!

Lesley Butcher
Lesley, you believed in this project from the first written word. I am so
grateful for your endless help, research, and support. Without you, this
book would look and feel very different, and I think every reader will
appreciate the difference you have made on this project. Thank you!

Paula Roach
In many ways, your example of love and commitment to the Lord, helped
me to know what to look for in a wife. Now I am forever grateful! Thanks
for being the greatest "sister" I could ever ask for!

Youth Source Team and Board

Your passion to encourage, instruct, equip, and inspire the youth pastors and leaders of this generation is unbelievable. Thanks for your commitment to me and for your desire to create excellent resources to help equip excellent leaders!

Dan Valentine

Dan, this book wouldn't have happened if it were not for you. Thanks, not only for the idea, but also for the confidence that I could pull it off. Thanks for believing in me and teaching me how to dream!

Jim Kochenburger

Thanks for giving this book a professional touch. I am so grateful for your help in making this book become a reality and something that I'm proud of.

Janet Angelo

Thanks for your professionalism and your desire to help craft this book into a wonderful resource for parents in ministry. You have done a wonderful job and I appreciate your heart for this project of mine.

Pastor and Mrs. Holden and The Harvest Time Team

Pastor Holden, I am so grateful for your love, support and leadership. You have believed in me and my dreams from day one. I feel it to be a great honor to associate myself with you and the Harvest Time family. There isn't another church and ministry team that I would rather "do life" with than Harvest Time. Thanks!

Craig and Sarah Johnson

For your friendship and support…now and tomorrow. I am the luckiest guy in the world to work with friends like you!

For my kid(s)…
May the title "Dad" always come before "Pastor."
You will always win.

For my Mom and Dad…
For everything…really…everything!

CHAPTER 1

Life Under The Microscope

Have you ever wanted to make yourself invisible? I have. One of those moments came as I was working at a ministry in Australia. It was a warm spring day, and the wind blowing off the ocean made me incredibly glad for the month I was spending in this Aussie paradise of sand and sea. I was glad, too, that I was far enough away from home that I could just be "Josh"—not "Josh Mayo, the pastor's kid." Now, don't get me wrong. I'm immeasurably proud of my parents and my Christian heritage. But growing up in a pastor's home, I learned that people almost unconsciously put expectations on you when they find out you're a "P.K." (pastor's kid).

Sadly enough, my blissful period of being "just another teenager" was short-lived. It was during my time there that I found myself amidst a bunch of ministry trainees. We had all shared generic information about ourselves; I hadn't said my last name so I didn't feel the need to worry. I consoled myself by thinking; *I'm thousands of miles away from home visiting friends in Australia. Now maybe I can finally be anonymous.*

The laughter and talk of the ministers-in-training seemed pretty typical. But then my ears tuned in as I heard a side conversation that included my parents' names. *Just a coincidence,* I assured myself. *Remember, Josh, you're on the other side of the world in*

Australia. Your season of being under the microscope has taken a temporary but much-needed reprieve.

My jaw tightened and my stomach knotted as I quickly realized that the "Sam and Jeanne Mayo" being discussed were in fact my parents after all. I could tell by the voice of the person speaking that he seemed to enjoy his juicy "new" information that he was now proclaiming. With a flash of anguish, I remembered that my mom had been the speaker for a national gathering of Australian youth pastors the year before. Unfortunately, my dream of getting out from under the microscope was coming to a screeching halt. But at that moment, I couldn't believe what I was hearing.

When I was growing up, my parents often told me that we can, in our carnal human nature, often try to tear other people down to make ourselves feel bigger or more important. Maybe that dynamic was at work that day. Whatever his reasoning may have been, this young man began to communicate with an air of confidence that left no one wondering whether he had his story straight or not. In a loud, stage-whisper voice, he encouraged the other youth pastors to "pray for the Mayo's." (Isn't it funny how most church gossip often begins as a prayer request?) He shared that my folks had been thrown out of their church in America. He went on to explain how he had heard that they'd done something "pretty bad."

I listened to his juicy melodrama until I felt the burning red flush of anger spread across my face, and then I cleared my throat, hoping that the lump I felt in my throat would give way as I tried to form words. My anger was obvious. The guy was lying—spreading a flat-out lie.

"If you don't mind," I heard myself interjecting, which caused the people who stood all around us to grow alert; "I couldn't help overhear your comments about the ministry couple in the U.S. and I'd like to bring some clarification to the story." The speaker glanced awkwardly in my direction, almost with a look of disappointment that his ministry horror story might be coming to a speedy close.

"You see," I continued, "I know the Mayos personally, and I think you've received some serious misinformation. Yes, they have recently left the church where they pastored for thirteen years. But they were definitely not 'thrown out.' They chose to leave and are accepting a pastorate in another city." The circle of ministers-in-training seemed almost frozen as I surveyed their faces for a response. "Besides that," I continued, "they are very much still in full-time ministry. They are as impassioned about the work of God as they have ever been. And most of all let me assure you as someone who lives very up-close to them, that there has been absolutely nothing inappropriate or questionable in their character whatsoever. They are people of the highest integrity." The silence that followed my heated words seemed to only punctuate my impassioned response. How dare this guy, thousands of miles from my home, try to rip my parents' reputation down with his garbled version of recent events. Suddenly, remaining anonymous was not nearly as important as setting the record straight.

Finally, the man nervously broke the tense silence. He shuffled his feet and appeared almost angry himself that his juicy story had been discredited, "How do you know that you've got *your* story straight?" He retorted back in my direction.

Well, here goes my dream of having a few weeks where people don't know me as a P.K., I thought to myself. But somehow, my intense loyalty to my parents made the decision to speak up in their defense an easy one.

"Well," I began my answer, looking the guy straight in the eye. "I'm very sure of my information, because they happen to be my parents. Any more questions, gentlemen?"

The group instantly began expressing their embarrassed apologies, almost stumbling over one another to do so. One guy even volunteered a condescending, "I knew that story couldn't be right about your parents" (a common follow-up phrase that ministers use to justify their current gossip). But as I walked away from their circle, my anger still burned. I was angry about the false rumors the guy had been communicating about my parents, but also as selfish as it might sound, I was also ticked-off that my shot at being out from underneath the "ministry microscope" for a few weeks had just gone down the drain. *So much for being just another kid,* I thought to myself. *Maybe the next time I want to be invisible, I should try taking a trip to Indonesia or something!*

Before I go on, let me set the story straight. I wasn't quite this bold in my actual response to those guys that day. But truth be known, they weren't quite as apologetic as I give them credit for either. Yet, the gist of the story remains painfully accurate, much like the glare of the microscope that most kids growing up in ministry families experience.

Living life under a social microscope isn't easy for anyone, much less a child in the ministry. Whether you're raising P.K.'s (pastor's kids), missionary kids, deacon/elder's kids, or your kids practically "live at the church," because you volunteer in a key ministry role, raising a child in this context is a very difficult and sometimes a scary challenge. The life of a child in the ministry has been described in many different ways. Authors Cameron Lee and Jack Balswick appropriately call it "life in a glass house."[1] Other writers describe it as living in a fishbowl. Regardless of the description, being in a ministry family is to be part of a culture all its own. I've grown to understand this culture very well, and yes, I've lived to tell about it.

Ministry Kids: The Upside, the Downside

Reverend Lester Sumrall, whose grandfather ministered both in the United States and overseas, remembers growing up with both his father and his grandfather in ministry. Of this he once said, "Everyone was constantly watching what I did. If I passed gas on one side of the building, it was reported to my grandfather by at least four o' clock that afternoon!"[2] Every P.K. would relate to this quote. We know what it is like to live a life "under the microscope."

Ask most children and teenagers whose parents are actively involved in the ministry and you will hear some common sentiments — both positive and negative. We conducted surveys with dozens of P.K.'s from different denominations, of different ages, and from different parts of the country. Some of the repeating themes from our surveys gave us great insight into some of the common threads that typically link all P.K.'s, helping us define this culture we've grown up in. Many of their quotes have helped me to add shape and insight to each chapter that follows. We hope that our insights will help you as parents in the ministry, which is why we so willingly gave our opinions. We really all just want to be understood.

Although you will see me use the term P.K. (pastor's kid) throughout this book, please understand that this book is written with the intent to give help to all parents who are actively raising their kids in the ministry. So whether your role in the church is that of full-time staff member or that of a priceless volunteer, this book is definitely for you.

Matt Swaggart, grandson of former televangelist Jimmy Swaggart, says, "If ministers have never been a P.K. themselves, they have no clue what it's like...it's a totally different world."[3] As a Christian leader (whether you are a pastor, missionary, youth leader, committed volunteer, etc.), you must realize that your children intuitively know that many sets of eyes are upon them continually. Few parents attempt to explain this unique social context to their children. No one really provides insights on how to help children navigate life as a P.K. That is what I hope this book will do.

Rebels or Models: The Expectation Trap

I remember years ago when my brother went through his own "grunge stage." Now, please know that my parents appreciated the financial savings that his obsessive shopping at thrift stores brought to the family budget, but at times, his crazy t-shirts, like the one that read, "Herman's Bar and Grill," caught my dad a little off guard.

My mom smilingly recalls the number of jabbing comments she experienced the year my brother bought his school overcoat at a thrift store. It was a bright yellow fireman's coat, trimmed in orange, which sported the name of its former owner, "Simpson," on its back. My brother chose to proudly wear this hard-to-miss coat at the height of the "preppy movement" in our Christian high school; maybe it was his way of letting others around him know that he simply refused to conform. Whatever the case, not until years later did we learn that my mom endured all sorts of comments about that coat from people on the school faculty and in the church.

What was the unspoken message? After all, teenagers from countless other homes around the school and church were taking their own jump into the grunge clothing movement, and no one seemed to give them much notice. But because Justin was a "P.K.," the expectations of others seemed to be very different. It was summed up well by one faculty member's chiding remark to my mom, "That coat just doesn't fit the mold of normal pastor's kid's clothing."

Whether it is fair or not, most kids who come from ministry families will tell you that there is an unspoken set of expectations that often seep into their lives as they're growing up. The lenses that these children are placed under serve one purpose – to magnify everything they do. They're expected to dress a certain way, talk a certain way, and act a certain way. For example, if a pastor's kid gets in trouble with friends, suddenly it is their fault for not doing the right thing. If a pastor's kid tears his jeans right before church, it's a shame he has to wear wholly jeans. If a pastor's kid doesn't do well on a test, suddenly he or she is the example to the entire class. So, what does all this say?

It says two things, some parents expect the pastors' kids to be models for their own children, whereas others assume they will be rebels without a cause. Both of these expectations can be a real trap for the P.K.—one is an impossible standard to live up to, and the other is a negative label they can't shake off; one that sadly can become a self-fulfilling prophecy.

Shared Frustrations and Appreciations

Listening to story after story, it becomes crystal clear that kids raised in the ministry have some of the same things in common—the same frustrations, the same hurts, and the same appreciation for life in the ministry. Interestingly enough, despite some of the pressures of living life "under the microscope," most children whose parents were deeply involved in ministry had far more positive things to say about the experience than negative. As these chapters unfold, it is my hope that the experiences described shed light on some of the more common "sinkholes" ministry families regularly face in "raising great kids while doing great ministry." I write this book so that these potential "sinkholes" might be strategically avoided in your families.

Heart to Heart: P.K. to Parent

This book comes straight to you from the heart of someone who has experienced the P.K. life firsthand. In it, also, are countless thoughts and stories from students whose parents are church volunteers, evangelists, missionaries, and pastors. Allow us to give you a behind-the-scenes look that will enhance your wisdom and perspective on how your kids may feel.

I want to help you set aside the secret fear that your son or daughter will grow up to be a "rebellious, non-Christian brat." Granted, there are some unique challenges of raising a son or daughter "in the fishbowl." But the rewards are ultimately far, far greater than any potholes in the road that you may encounter.

Parenting 101!

I heard a speaker on parenting once say, "When a child reaches 13, it would be best if you built a box for him, cut a hole in it, and then put the teenager inside the box for safe keeping. Then when the child reaches the age of 16, *plug up the hole!"* Humorous as this story is, it reflects the honest fear many parents experience when it comes to raising their children in the best way possible. Congratulations on being someone who has gone beyond your fears and has decided to take action on becoming a more effective parent. Not only did it take some bravery on your part to not only purchase this book, but also to take the time to actually read it!

Let's face it. Most leaders in the church world today went to university or seminary to learn skills to prepare them for some form of ministry. Yet, few of them ever had the slightest instruction on how to be a parent—let alone how to parent kids who will be under the microscope continually. As someone once said, "Parents are just kids who grew up and had kids." So, is it possible to be a successful minister and parent at the same time? The answer is yes, of course.

"True success in ministry is when those who know me best... love me most."

This is my mom's definition of success, and through the years I've heard her say it countless times. Growing up, I would hear other preacher's kids complain how their parents did not live out at home what they loudly proclaimed in church. I must admit, I've often felt very fortunate on this count. I sometimes felt a little guilty because I didn't have any "sad stories" like that to tell. My dad and mom have lived out this definition of success, and I'll stack it up against any one else's concept of ministry success. I can say without hesitation that both of my parents have been unbelievably successful in the ministry. If only this quote could become a more widely used scale for measuring success!

What many congregations, television audiences, youth ministries, and radio listeners don't understand is that in the privacy of the home, sometimes these revered men and women of God are more human than most people realize. They may have incredible life experiences, spiritual anointing, and doctoral degrees, but rarely have any of them taken a class on how to raise godly children, and beyond that, how to do so while lots of people are watching.

Realize your kids are in a position of privilege...and scrutiny.

Few people understand all of the dynamics behind raising a child while being heavily involved in some form of ministry. Psychologists compare the family of a minister to one of Europe's "royal families." The father and mother are equated to being like a king and queen whose children are born into a life of both privilege and scrutiny. But as it is with a king or queen, no matter how they portray themselves to be among the people, there is an invisible line that divides the two. Children of Christian leaders will inevitably incur scrutiny as well as be offered many privileges. Both of these must be acknowleged.

P.K.'s learn to love the ministry life or to hate it.

As parents, you have the awesome privilege of creating an environment where your kids will thrive in God's kingdom rather than resent it. Many P.K.'s like myself honestly grew up believing that this life was a privilege. But that attitude didn't just happen. It took work to look beyond the scrutiny to see the privilege.

Satan has placed a target on your kids...make sure he misses.

There is probably no area where parents are more vulnerable to attack than through the lives of their children. Thus, it is little wonder that the enemy, Satan, often targets his most brutal assaults in the direction of a minister's family. Your children are not just your offspring. They are a part of the total you (including your ministry). And rest assured, the enemy does not take them lightly.

Ideally, all parents should have a strategic game plan before their first child arrives on the scene. But proactive parenting is pr~'

ably more of a great concept than a frequently practiced lifestyle. Throughout the course of this book, I hope to encourage the use of a proactive parenting process no matter where you might be in relationship to raising your family.

Through these chapters you will discover a few boundaries you can set, a few principles you can live by, and a few tangible practices that will help you navigate through the parenting journey from the perspective of a P.K. as you also fulfill God's ministry calling on your life. Most importantly, I pray that through these chapters you will receive renewed faith that your child does not need to fall victim to the stereotype of being a "rebellious kid raised in the ministry."

We've all heard the stories and probably know a few of our own firsthand. Perhaps that is why so many men and women in ministry have come to my parents and asked, "Talk to us ... Tell us how your kids turned out so well? How did you balance being full-time parents with being full-time ministers?"

Of course, I am unashamedly partial to my parents, Sam and Jeanne Mayo. As their son, I can tell you firsthand that they did an amazing job balancing the demands of raising my brother and me while also serving God wholeheartedly in full-time ministry. Yes, I know I'm a little biased, nevertheless I honestly believe that they are about as close to the ideal of "parenting perfection" as one will ever find.

Yet, with all they did right, they would be quick to disagree with me and give you a list of "all the things we could have done better." Someone once said, "There is absolutely no way to be a perfect parent. There are, however, a million ways to be a good one." My parents focused more on priorities than on perfection, and I believe that made all the difference.

I've taken a mental journey back through my growing up years to try to dissect some of the reasons why things turned out as well as they did for me. So, on behalf of your child, thanks for caring enough about your family (or future family) to read a book like this one. After all, *God Jehovah was a FATHER even before He was a CREATOR.* That gives us a mighty powerful look at His priorities.

THINK ABOUT IT...

In the upcoming chapters you will find "think about it" questions designed to help you easily consider how some of the information in each chapter applies to your personal situation. Let's be honest with each other. We have seen sections like these in many books before, but our typical habit is to skip over them to just get on to the next chapter. I really want to encourage you to take that extra moment of time to ponder these questions and evaluate your family's application of the material.

CHAPTER 2

A Parent's Moment To Count The Cost

Dear Pastor, as a P.K., if I could tell you one thing…
It's an amazing thing to have children, but please take the time to plan ahead and prepare, because your kids really will deal with life differently. - Lesley (Piersall) Butcher[4]

For many people the heavy responsibilities of home and family and earning a living absorb all their time and strength. Yet such a home – where love is – may be a light shining in a dark place, a silent witness to the reality and the love of God. – Olive Wyon[5]

My parents encountered many challenges not long after I was born. For the first two years of my life they checked me in and out of hospitals, allowing countless medical procedures to determine why I couldn't gain any weight. My parents stood firm as they prayed and believed for my healing while the days, weeks, and months rolled by.

At the peak of my illness, only 24 hours after the doctors told my parents that I was "starving to death," my father had preached an impassioned message entitled, "Christ Is Our Healer." Nightly, my mom slept on the floor under my baby bed in the hospital's pediatric division. She begged the Lord to allow her to take the pain of the continual needles and tests rather than her treasured firstborn son. All of my parents' idealistic dreams of easy, just "sing a lullaby" parenting had come to a screeching halt.

To make matters worse, some fellow Christians were adding to my parents' pain. Led by false teaching, these people had concluded there could only be one of two reasons I had not yet been healed: first, my parents were not people of faith (because if they were, my healing would have manifested by this point), or second; my parents had some form of hidden sin in their lives. These individuals believed God was not answering my parents' prayers because of some form of secret sin or uncovered deceit in their own personal walks with Him. The sustained strain of those 24 months was excruciating.

The turning point in my medical situation came approximately two years later when the Lord graciously began a slow but non-glamorous healing process, enabling me to assimilate nutrition from my food.

When you first become a parent, you accept every present and future responsibility and trial that it will bring. It's impossible to know what will be expected of you in the years that follow, but your commitment to your child is much like the commitment you made on your wedding day—for better or for worse.

Parenting Tests and Trials Turned to Gold

I Peter 1:7 tells us that pure gold put in the fire comes out of it proved pure; genuine faith put through this suffering comes out proved genuine.[6] When Jesus wraps this all up, it's your faith — and not your gold — that God will have on display as evidence of His victory. Through the fires of life and circumstances, you too will endure tests that will try you and mold you into the man or woman of God He has called you to be. If you are a typical parent, you will find that the trials which impact your children are among the most difficult for you to endure.

Satan knew from the beginning of time that a strategic spot of attack in the heavenly Father's heart was on that of His "only begotten Son." So, it is little wonder why the enemy's attack on Jesus was so unrelenting. Some might say that the Son was the Father's ultimate point of vulnerability.

How deep is your personal commitment to trust and live the Word of God? That trust will undoubtedly be tested through the lives of your most treasured possessions, your children. One once said that, "He who would make bread for others, must first himself go through the mill." Apart from these testing times, perhaps many of us would become proud, legalistic, and untouchable in our ministries, making it very difficult to relate to others. Our answers would become trite and superficial. Our sermons might become laced with cheap formulas and sayings. Even the divine Son Himself "faced all the temptations we do" (Hebrews 4:15)[7]. The depth of His ministry came, at least in part, from His choice to feel what we feel and suffer like we suffer. Thankfully, our wise heavenly Father values our character above our comfort.

Along the road of parenting, expect your faith to be challenged repeatedly. Your commitment to live by the principles and promises in the Word of God will provide countless opportunities for you to be tested and strengthened. Why? Perhaps it is because true faith trusts the character of God even when we do not fully understand His actions.

Parental Trials Keep Faith Real

Through the years, I've repeatedly heard people graciously describe the ministry of Sam and Jeanne Mayo (my parents) as "believable and easily received." I belive one reason for this is that some of the challenges of raising children helped to keep them in touch with real life, real pain, and real faith.

Counting the Cost

Dear Pastor, as a P.K., if I could tell you one thing…

Ask for wisdom about the money situation, what and how much you will need. - Anonymous P.K.

One thing I didn't like about growing up in the ministry was the tight financial strain. - Anonymous P.K.

It has been observed that people often put more thoughtful planning into purchasing a new car than weighing all factors involved in effective parenting. My parents often quote the scripture from Luke 14:28 that says, "Don't begin until you count the cost. For who would begin construction of a building without first getting estimates and then checking to see if there is enough money to pay the bills?"[8] Before we start building a life, we must stop and count the cost as well—or risk years of frustration and confusion. The "costs" that need to be counted include not only areas of finance, but also time, emotional demands, and much more.

A proactive plan is needed to face the many new changes and conflicts that come with raising children. Here are a few specific things my parents did to "count the cost" before my brother and I were born:

Be willing to wait.

From day one, my parents knew they wanted to work in ministry together. Long before I was ever born, they left a ministry in Georgia and accepted the position as senior pastor of a church in Bellevue, Nebraska. They began the work with great anticipation, yet with only a small congregation and an even smaller budget. They realized the church needed both of them full-time to get it off the ground, and the time commitment was great. In response to this demand, my parents decided to wait five years before starting a family.

As I talked to my mom years later about this decision, she responded by saying, "We wanted to give ourselves time to establish the ministry there in Bellevue but not neglect future responsibilities to our children." So with the Lord's help, they delayed their parenting years for a short time to make sure they could do both worlds equal justice. The "when to have children" question is obviously a very important part of counting the cost.

Grow your marriage first, then your family.

Besides wanting to establish the ministry in Nebraska, my parents counted the cost and decided they wanted to grow their marriage before they faced the challenge of growing their family. Obviously, though, even with great planning, "surprises" can arrive on the scene in the best of marriages. When this occurs, every ministry couple is able to rest in the awareness that there are no surprises from the Lord's perspective. It's been said, "Where the Lord *guides,* He *provides,*" and how very true that is in the life-altering role of parenthood.

Choose a desired future over a desired present.

In addition to emotionally preparing for children, financial preparation is equally as critical. Sometimes we must forfeit a desired present to create a desired future. For many of us, a desired present involves the luxury of all the "toys" our society so prioritizes. You know what they are: sharp car, luxurious home, beautiful furnishings, expensive clothing, and more. We cannot fulfill these present desires if it means contributing to the detriment of our time, finances and energy that could be going towards creating a stronger foundation and future for our children. Our unbridled desires often tempt us to obtain in the first three to five years of our marriage the same lifestyle that our parents worked decades to achieve. This is an economic recipe for disaster. Even more, it is a recipe for family stress in huge ways. When the reality of heavy indebtedness begins to sink in, our children often become the ones who suffer the most.

New Car or Nanny Fund?

While serving in Nebraska, my parents drove an old, beat-up silver car. It was the kind of car you heard a block away, and every time you placed the key in the ignition, it took sheer faith to believe it would start. The features that my parents best recall were the rust spots deteriorating away at the body of the car they fondly called "The Beast." Many cold winters in Nebraska were spent hoping "The Beast" would start. Even when it did, there was still the issue of the passenger window that refused to close completely.

Despite the sincere need to upgrade the vehicle to something more reliable and attractive, my parents chose not to upgrade their vehicle for quite some time. You see, they knew that they were hoping to become parents within the next couple of years. Thus, instead of putting money aside to purchase another car, they began "the nanny fund." Allow me to share my parents' perspective on this decision.

Even before I arrived on the scene, my mom and dad both felt very deeply that my mother was to remain actively involved in youth ministry. My mom often told herself, "The President of the United States has no more time in his day than I do. So with careful planning, I will be able to fulfill my desire to be one of the world's greatest moms while still being significantly involved in ministry." After thought and prayer, my parents decided that a part-time nanny would help to pragmatically make both worlds possible. Through different seasons in our lives, this young woman was in our home for varying amounts of time, ranging from approximately 6 hours a week to a full forty hours a week.

Granted, the aging silver Toyota "Beast" continued to be a driving challenge and a source of embarrassment to my parents. But as a part of this "counting the cost" principle, they realized that their future firstborn son would never be impacted by their pride-busting old car. In contrast, they knew that I would be very impacted by the amount of personal time my mother would be able to spend with me, even as a young baby. So, instead of being bogged down with household chores, our nanny helped eliviate much of the work so that we could have more family time.

The "nanny" was usually a young college woman involved in our youth ministry. Mom hired her to come during key times in the day when I would often be napping. She not only watched over me during these times but also carried out a specific list of house-keeping responsibilities.

My mom laughingly recalls, "It was another pride-buster to have someone else folding your husband's underwear! But I realized that most of my time-management was going to boil down to a series of exchanges. I could either use my hours at home playing with my children or cleaning my bathrooms. Only I could decide."

As the years progressed, the number of hours that the nanny spent in our home increased, reaching approximately 40 hours a week before I entered kindergarten. Though most families would not need this much assistance, even a few hours of help twice a week could make an immeasurable difference.

The Price of Parenting

Counting the cost is significant and applicable. Whether your child is still unborn or is a demanding teenager, consider taking some time to journal some of the "price-tags" you believe are associated with the kind of positive parenting you want to provide. What will some of these decisions cost you – emotionally, financially, and in regards to your schedule? Then prayerfully ask the Lord to help you come up with a clear plan of attack for responding to those price tags. Just a little hint as you begin to think, the most important cost factors will involve either your calendar or your wallet. So take some time to be strategic in these arenas and your children will later thank you.

With careful planning, someone could be brought into the home just once or twice a week to allow a "ministry mom" an afternoon of ministry outside the home with no apprehension or guilt. Sometimes the Lord even provides a person from the congregation who is willing to consistently volunteer a couple of hours on a specific day of each week. Thoughtful planning can help you prioritize a desired future goal over an impulsive present desire, making all the difference for your family.

THINK ABOUT IT...

1. Every stage of parenting has different types of "counting the cost" moments. Sometimes the cost involves emotional price tags rather than finances or time. Reflect for a few minutes on some of the specific price tags that you think might be most important to pay the price for in regards to your family's situation right now.

2. There is an old expression that simply says, "Pay now ... or pay later." Motivate yourself to thoughtfully "count the cost" by taking time to reflect on what the toll on your family may be later if you are not willing to begin paying a few specific prices now.

3. Bring to mind someone you respect as a parent. Ask them to share with you some of the specific "prices" they have paid, which they felt were very pivotal in their parenting.

**Dad and Mom on their wedding day and
the beginning of my family**

Mom and I share a laugh even despite how crazy life felt in and out of the hospital

**Me playing in the snow with Tamara –
my "big sister" and nanny**

CHAPTER 3

Not To Decide...Is To Decide

My dad was very involved and cares a lot about the church, and I just felt I wasn't spending any alone time with him. I really didn't get to know him...I still don't. – Vanessa Cobbs[9]

My parents were very deliberate in the way they raised us.
– Marcus Haggard[10]

Imagine a little girl sitting outside on a sidewalk. She is carefully drawing lines on the pavement as if she was playing a game all by herself. Another child approaches her and gives her a questioning look. "Why are you drawing lines and mumbling to yourself? No one is here yet." "I know," answers the first little girl confidently. "But if I draw the lines and make up the rules before they come, I know I'll be sure to win!"

If you want to be a great parent while still being significantly involved in ministry, you will be wise to take time to draw the lines and write the rules now so you can "be sure to win." Around the Mayo home, we reference this kind of thinking as making "pre-choice choices." This strategic "Mayo-ism" simply means to determine key decisions in one's future, which will have significant implications. Then, after "counting the cost," making a decision beforehand of how you will choose to respond. By doing this, we enable ourselves to set Christ-honoring boundaries and to eliminate much confusion—particularly at key turning points in our lives.

Protect Your Priorities

The types of "pre-choice choices" my parents made while raising my brother and me changed often through the years. But they wisely thought through those choices before they found themselves "under the gun" and reacting to the pressure of the moment. My father would often comment that without making some important pre-choice choices the most precious people in one's life would be those most easily violated.

Perhaps one of the most strategic "pre-choice choices" came in the area of my parent's ministry travel schedules. Through the years, my father elected to decline most "away" speaking invitations in order to fulfill the demanding role of senior pastor. But Mom was becoming a leader nationally in the field of youth ministry. She laughingly says that since most youth pastors only average 18 months in one location, it did not take much giftedness to become somewhat of a leader in the field. Thus, prior to my arrival on the scene, Mom was traveling two to three times a month in ministry commitments away from our church. Dad was her biggest cheerleader, feeling that her ministry gifts for speaking and being a youth leadership coach were needed nationally.

The Price of Pre-Choice Choices

Before I was born, my parents realized that my mother's traveling schedule needed to slow down dramatically in order for her to be the kind of parent she wanted to be. As they reflected on some of their earlier "pre-choice choices," mom fondly references this area as one of her most strategic choices. After talking things over, they made the decision to limit her away ministry to a maximum of two days per month. Thus, for the next 21 years (the time needed to get both my younger brother and myself out of high school), my parents' decision in this area held firm. Once those two days a month were committed, there were no more decisions to be made. No matter how large, flattering, or exciting the ministry invitation might be, her decision was already made. My parents had made a pre-choice choice.

With a mixture of amusement and astonishment, my brother and I would sometimes kid with Mom about this as we got older. Repeatedly, she turned down international ministry opportunities because the mere travel time ruled out the opportunity in her mind. Looking back now, I remember as teenagers in high school how often Justin and I told her to "think again" when she turned down invitations to exciting places like Australia (a place we both desperately wanted to visit). But these kinds of consistent priority calls sent a loud and unmistakable message to both of us as we were growing up. Our parents were far more interested in being heroes to us than to the rest of the world.

Years later, my brother and I recall overhearing Mom once again starting to decline another opportunity to minister at a key Australian youth leader's event. We reminded her that by the arrival of the proposed ministry date, both of us would have graduated and would probably no longer be living at home. In short, we reminded her that during the upcoming season in her life, she could "break her rule without breaking her commitment to the family." Thus, after declining several invitations to speak at the event, she finally accepted the invitation. (Want to smile? I arranged my schedule so I could go with her to Australia!)

As you read these pages, stop momentarily to decide vital places where you need to make some pre-choice choices in your own parenting. The Word of God says that a "double-minded man is unstable in all his ways." So are double-minded parents! So whatever the age of your son or daughter, determine appropriate places where you are going to "draw the lines and write the rules." In doing so, you will help to insure that one day you will be certain to win in the strategic game of parenting.

Have an S.I.P. (System in Place)
Dear Pastor: As a P.K., if I could tell you one thing…

May your job never look more important than your kids…love them more than the ministry…Spend more focused time with them than your next counseling appointment. - Anonymous P.K.

If you want to get something done in the ministry, you need to have an S.I.P. This simple but important concept began for me a couple of years ago when several of my ministry friends were trying to figure out an answer to a problem. One of them finally spoke up and said that we needed an S.I.P. – a system in place. If we had a system in place, issues could be quickly resolved when they arose. In the same way, you have to develop ministry S.I.P.'s.

Part of what makes ministry so different from other occupations is that it is far from a typical nine-to-five job. Ministry often requires extra time during the evenings and on weekends, times when most families are enjoying time together. Even beyond the "family-time" which is forfeited for ministry, children with parents in ministry often complain about the amount of time they are forced to spend on church property. One of the P.K.'s we surveyed commented, "I never felt like I had a real home. I was either asleep in my bed or asleep in a pew at church. It was all the same to me."[11] Even when church schedules seem out of hand, there has got to be a system in place.

The Sunday and Wednesday Night Aunt and Uncle
My parents wanted to make sure that we grew up loving the house of the Lord rather than resenting the fact that we spent so many hours there. This was definitely a situation where a system in place was needed. What was the S.I.P. you might ask? We just called it our "Sunday and Wednesday night aunt and uncle."

I still remember our first after-church aunt and uncle. This amazing couple was Dennis and Peggy Bradbury. Our parents knew that Sunday and Wednesday nights could be very long ones for us at church, due to people who legitimately needed to speak with them or receive ministry. But they did not want my brother and I "trapped" after service, waiting for them to conclude the evening's ministry. They understood youthful impatience and decided to create a solution for the problem before it affected our attitudes toward church.

The Bradburys were a loving, older couple who were a part of our church in Nebraska. My parents talked with them privately, sharing the depth of their commitment to preserve their sons' positive attitudes toward the Lord's house. They asked this fun-loving older couple if they would consider becoming our "adopted aunt and uncle" on Sunday and Wednesday evenings after church concluded. They presented this role as the strategic ministry that they truly believed it to be. The Bradburys were simply asked to pick us up right after church each Sunday and Wednesday evening and take us home.

The Bradburys not only had a key to our home, but they also had an understanding of the childhood rituals that characterized bedtime for Justin and me. Above that, they were warm, loving people that we grew to love being around. Thus, this simple but strategic S.I.P. reduced to almost zero the times that the Mayo boys "got stuck" at church. My parents helped wonderful people like the Bradburys to consider this role as a genuine extension of their ministry; and so it was.

My family exchanged Christmas and birthday gifts with them through the years because they were so much more than "babysitters." They became loving extensions of our family. Occasionally, when Justin or I had a minor illness that prevented us from attending church, the Bradburys came to our home to make sure my parents could go to church with peace of mind, knowing we were in good, loving hands.

The Importance of Having a S.I.P.

As the years passed, older teenagers from the youth ministry became "adopted big brothers and sisters" for us and fulfilled some of the same functions. It became a great way for us, as young boys, to have a few consistent teenage role models we could look up to while also making sure we never felt "trapped" in the house of the Lord.

I recall hearing my parents say something like, "We're happy to minister to everyone else's family... just as long as our own family doesn't get the raw end of the deal." So by cultivating some of these adopted "aunts, uncles, and big brothers" through the years, my parents were able to put a system in place that assured the best for their own family.

Interestingly enough, by having great people like the Bradburys in our lives, my brother and I weren't the only ones who benefited. While my mom and dad remained at church, their minds could stay completely focused on praying for and listening to others. They didn't have to look around, wondering if my brother and I were ok, or feel guilty that they were keeping us out late. As pastors, they ministered to members of the congregation and then gave members of our congregation concrete ways that they could minister to us as a family.

It Takes a Village...

An old African proverb says, "It takes a village to raise a child."[12] With some thoughtful pre-planning and sincere appreciation, the local body of Christ can become a loving "village" that helps to fill your son or daughter's life with countless positive, fun memories. Prayerfully choose those who you want to help be a part of raising your children. Encourage them both inside and outside the church. Be clear that you view their role as a ministry and not as a baby-sitting service. Your children will one day be sincerely grateful to you for thinking ahead. I know I am.

He who spends the most time ... wins.

Parents are prone to give their children everything except the one thing they need most. That is time. - Emma K. Hubburt[13]

Dear Pastor, as P.K., if I could tell you one thing...

Always remember that a balance of unconditional love, discipline, and time are three most crucial elements.

– Kellie (Berteau) Williams[14]

Dear Pastor, as a P.K., if I could tell you one thing...

Do not let your ministry take the place of your family time. Always make time for family time, no matter what. - Z.H.[15]

For years, as my family has mentored others in the process of disciple-making, we have said, "He who spends the most time wins." And fortunately, my parents realized that their most focused "disciple-making" needed to be in the lives of their own children. Justin and I always knew that we never had to "fight for time" with our parents. Looking back now, I cannot imagine how difficult it must have been, but they consistently made sure that their time priorities backed up their words. They truly loved us...not just with their words, but also with their time.

Quality Time vs. Quantity of Time

Simplistic as the concept may be, it will be impossible to counteract the pressures of life under the ministry microscope without a prioritized effort on your part to spend both quality and quantity time with your children. No son or daughter wants to feel like they get the "emotional leftovers" of a busy parent in the ministry. Candidly, I believe that this lack of meaningful, focused time is perhaps some of the most fertile ground for resentment that the enemy, Satan, cultivates.

Years ago, well-intentioned ministers would attempt to ease their guilty consciences by quoting phrases like, "It's not the quantity of time spent with your children, but rather, the quality." Unfortunately, Satan has happily anointed distortions like these, knowing full-well how helpful they would be for his hell-bent cause.

Psalm 90:12 says, "Teach us to make the most of our time, so that we may grow in wisdom." [16] Our children will probably not grow up wishing that we had given them more toys or allowed them to do more fun things. Our children will, however, look back and wish we had spent more time with them. In today's society, I think we all recognize our time to be an even more valuable "currency" than our finances. As challenging as it may seem, we must strategically plan ways to insure that our own children get large amounts of meaningful time ... not because they are our "projects," but because they are our priorities.

What P.K.'s dislike most about their parents being in ministry ...

In an anonymous survey, we asked nearly a hundred P.K.'s what they *disliked most* about their parents being significantly involved in the ministry.[17] Not surprisingly, one of the most repeated complaints centered on this strategic time issue. Here is a sampling of the most common responses:

- The time commitment – their parents needing to be available 24/7
- Ministry parents being gone on ministry trips a lot
- Having to share their family with others
- Lack of family time
- Not having their father home very much
- Feeling like their requests for their parents' time would be treated like just another duty their ministry parents would try to squeeze into their busy schedules

- Knowing that in the name of ministry, the family plans would be postponed or shortened.
- Feeling stupid and guilty for wanting their parents to take time to do the non-spiritual "parent things" that make kids feel normal (i.e. ball games and Girl Scouts)

100% at Home

How do you make time for those who are so important to you when the demands on you are so overwhelming? How do you make the best of what little time you do have? The only way to answer these questions is through a strategic plan. No one is asking you to give up the call of God upon your life and stay home all the time. But after dealing with all the counseling sessions, budget issues, member complaints, and leadership challenges of the church world, it is genuinely hard to have the emotional energy to truly "*be*" at home when you come home.

Hannah (Conneely)[18] relates, "When you hear the frightening, unbelievable stories of the pastor's daughter who got pregnant or the P.K. who ended up a drug addict, people always seem so shocked. And when the obvious questions are asked, such as 'How did this happen? How did they end up like this?' the children simply reply, 'Mom and Dad were never home. '"

The Church: Friend or Foe?

The son or daughter of a businessman or woman may fight a company for their parents' time, but P.K.'s feel that if they fight the church or ministry for time, it's the same as fighting God. Church and ministry are unmistakably all connected to God, and P.K.'s know they don't want to fight God. So out of reverence for Him and respect for your ministry, most of the time they'll just stop fighting. They will let you win. The last thing you want is for your kids to feel like your ministry is more important to you than they are. You don't want them to conclude that your ministry is their enemy. You especially don't want them to feel their enemy is God, when in all realty it is just your poor job of time-management.

A famous sculptor, Sir Jacob Epstein, once kept a huge block of stone in a corner. For weeks he planned how he would begin sculpting it. When a well-known author and friend, George Bernard Shaw, came to visit and asked why the stone was still in the corner, Epstein replied, "I don't know yet. I'm still making plans." Shaw replied with surprise, "You mean you plan your work. I change my mind several times a day!" The wise sculptor looked at him and said, "That's all very well with a four-ounce manuscript…but not with a four-ton block."[19]

Many aspects of your job may not require months of planning, and you may have the luxury of changing your mind numerous times a day. But as a parent, your children are far more important than an isolated counseling session or a bulletin insert. The need to put a strategy in place will protect you from all the little, negotiable areas that inevitably drain your time. You cannot predict every single step, but you can successfully keep your steps on the right path.

THINK ABOUT IT…

1. Think about some areas in your parenting which become confusing and frustrating for you. How might a "pre-choice choice" go a long way toward removing some of your future confusion and frustration?

2. When we give invitations to receive Christ at the close of a message, we sometimes say, "Not to decide… is to decide." Stop for a moment to determine a few areas where this would also be true concerning the raising of your children. An example of not clearly "deciding" might look something like not bringing to a close a counseling appointment that is now cutting into your pre-planned time with your children.

3. After making some "pre-choice choices," you may need to create and implement a few S.I.P.'s. Considering that your family time must be a priority, what systems do you feel would help your family understand that they take precedence over church-related business both inside and outside of the home?

Quality time with Mom

Quality time with Dad

CHAPTER 4

Crucial Battle Lines And Loving Boundaries

Draw clear battle lines where the ministry ends and family begins. – Annonymous P.K.

I have heard it suggested that all pastors should ask themselves an important question: "Am I embezzling time from my family?" He knew that another pastor could replace him at the church, but no one could replace him as a husband, father, and pastor in his own home.

You need to set the right kind of loving boundaries. These boundaries protect you from missing out on some of the most important moments of your child's life. There definitely is a war over the spiritual destiny of your child, and if you don't create some strategic boundaries, Satan eventually will. These boundaries add to a successful strategy in raising your child within the ministry. Many wise parents, including my own, have decided that they would mark out the boundaries before the first shot was ever fired. Once you're in the midst of the war, marking out the boundaries and drawing battle lines becomes impossible.

Prioritizing your time and evaluating your priorities is a lifestyle, not something that happens overnight. While looking at your day planner, remember to ask yourself this question, "Am I embezzling time from my family?"

In ministry and in life, the success of your future will always be hidden in the habits of your daily routine. Allow me to share six specific boundaries that my parents created that led to their success in raising my brother and me.

Loving Boundary #1 – Be home more often than you're away.
Dear Pastor, as a P.K., if I could tell you one thing…

Be home more and spend more time with us… become our best friend. - John Daugherty[20]

The kids all huddled around the phone to talk to their dad who'd been away ministering overseas for several weeks. After they'd all said their goodbyes and I love you's, Hannah, the youngest, was the last to hang up the phone. For weeks she hadn't been herself, but now she was back to being her same, always-smiling self. Her mom couldn't help but wonder what brought about the change. "Hannah why are you so happy?" she asked. Hannah's eyes grew wide as she looked up at her mom with the innocence of a four-year-old and said, "My daddy's coming home to visit."

It's a sobering moment when suddenly you're forced to view your lifestyle through the eyes of your children. I pray your heart shudders at the thought of your home being perceived by them as a place you visit, not the place where you really live.

You can say you love your children all day long, but they hear it most loudly through your actions. Most men and women in ministry assertively declare from the pulpit that their children and family take priority over their ministry, but in their homes, it really is a different story.

One of the best things you can do for your children is to provide them with childhood memories that include you. My mom and dad made sure they were only gone three key nights a week. Two of these obviously included Sunday and Wednesday nights for church services, and the third was reserved for a date night between just the two of them.

I know that the demands on men and women in ministry are enormous. There are board meetings, women's conferences, counseling appointments, dinner with other ministers, and the list goes on. If you want to assure spending time with your children, you have to schedule them in like you would anyone else.

When things come up, as they always do, those hours in your planner will have your children written all over them. Make it clear to others and your family that those four nights of the week are taken, and stand by your rule. If an extremely important opportunity presents itself, this is when it becomes the hardest.

Let's take a look at a few different scenarios:

Scenario #1:

A woman enters your office needing you to counsel her son for a few hours that evening. You look at your calendar and realize tonight is Thursday – your weekly game night with the kids. You express your concern to the woman, and ask her if you can schedule an appointment later because you have made prior commitments. Your kids win.

Scenario #2:

Your administrative assistant sends you a memo that an evangelist is going to be in from out of town and would like to get together for dinner. Your son has a soccer game, but you know you can make it to another one. Later that night you find out he scored his first goal, but it's too late. You decide you'll make sure you take him out for pizza the next week.

When you give up time to be with your family, you lose time you can never gain back. Giving your family four nights a week shows them that they mean more to you than the rest of the world and ensures that you are the primary spiritual influences in their lives. Even the most well meaning and spiritually anointed parents can lose the respect and admiration of their children through repeated disappointments and broken promises.

Emergencies inevitably arise, as there may be times when you have to let go of one of those four key nights a week, but your goal should be that those times are rare exceptions. What are you missing out on? Do your kids feel like you "*end up*" with them at the end of the day or that you're "*coming home*" *to them* at the end of the day?

My brother and I may not have fully appreciated the sacrifices our parents made to be home with us, and your children may not do so either for a long time, but may they reflect on their childhood days much like Ted Haggard's son Marcus:

> "We grew up with the impression that dad was always trying to get home. He made us feel like he was getting through everything else as quickly as he could so he could spend time with us. If he couldn't be with us right then, *we always knew he wanted to.*"[21]

Principle #1: You cannot replace a promised night with a future night. Make sure that not being home on key nights is the exception to the rule.

Loving Boundary #2: Make Big Events a Big Deal
Dear Pastor, as a P.K., if I could tell you one thing ...

My dad made his schedule around what we were doing... even if it's a basketball game, your kids need to know they're important!

- Matt Swaggart[22]

Dear Pastor, as a P.K., if I could tell you one thing…

Don't put ministry before your kids, even if it means letting go of something great or not getting to meet another minister or speak at a conference. - Ruth (Daugherty) Sanders[23]

When exceptions come, and time is sacrificed, there must be certain things that are non-negotiable. Big events such as birthdays, championship sports games, and holidays must not be missed. My parents never missed a big event. I know you're nodding and thinking, "I wouldn't dream of missing Rachel's game or Matthew's birthday." Any parent would have a hard time denying this, but it's amazing and ironic how many men and women in ministry have been offered their "greatest" speaking opportunity on days that mean so much to their families.

When opportunity knocks, be sure priorities answer.

Consciously realize that a window for the enemy to allow bitterness and resentment to come into the lives of your children may be disguised as a door of opportunity for your ministry. As children we don't remember the huge event you spoke at, nor do we recall the nationally respected evangelist you sat with on stage. We remember the game you missed or the birthday party you didn't make.

Years ago my father served as the Assistant Superintendent of the Nebraska District of the Assembly of God, and he had to attend a long business meeting that was more than 150 miles away. The first day of the meetings happened to be the same day as one of my soccer games, but when I looked to the sidelines while running down the field, who did I see cheering loudly for me? My mom and dad were there sitting side by side. My dad had to drive back to the meeting that same night, but his time and sacrifice made me feel that who I was and what I did mattered more. He may never know how greatly his sacrifice impacted my view of his love.

My parents aren't the only ones who recognize the importance of this concept of making it to the big events, regardless of what it costs. One nationally recognized evangelist's son proudly said, "Sure, my dad traveled and preached, but every year when basketball season started, he built his schedule around mine. He made sure that he never missed a game."

I had the privilege of interning under Richard Crisco, who at the time, was the head youth pastor at Brownsville Assembly of God. This church experienced a historic revival in the mid-1990s. Millions came to the church in Pensacola, Florida, accompanied by massive amounts of media and visits from other well-known ministers. Richard, along with others on the ministry staff, was pushed into an intense spotlight almost overnight. During this time the thing that mattered greatly to Richard was not that his name was respected throughout households in America, but that his name was loved and respected in his household. On one particular evening, he gave up being at a very significant event held at the church to be a part of his daughter's 15th birthday party. I'm sure eyebrows were raised as people questioned why he missed out on an important night at the church, but I know his answer would have been, "My daughter only turns fifteen once."

Similar stories from from P.K.'s seem endless. One son, whose parents traveled and performed dramas around the nation, remembers how the travel would come to a halt because his dad was committed to coaching his baseball team. This P.K. is now a husband and father with a family of his own, and he remembers what meant the most to him then. "My dad was my baseball coach for years, he never missed a game, and that was the coolest thing in the world to me."

Your children are only children once.

My mom came to numerous field trips and school functions when I knew she must be far busier than the other moms. The truth was, she held down far more responsibility than 99% of the other moms of kids in my class with her traveling ministry, her duties as a full-time youth pastor, and Christian school superintendent filling up her schedule. But she made time for the PTA meetings, the soccer games, the bake sales, and the senior trips. Continue to uphold the motto; "Your children are only children once." Significant moments hold more weight than we realize at the time they are happening. By making the big events a big deal, you avoid serious wounds and unhappy memories. You would be surprised how many big events are remembered as...*the one my mom or dad missed.*

Principle #2: Big events can either score big points or leave big wounds with your children.

Loving Boundary #3 – Disconnect the telephone.
Don't allow your home phone number to be given out, so people aren't calling you at 3 a.m. in the morning. - Anonymous P.K.

Dear Pastor, as a P.K., if I could tell you one thing…
Be the example of a good parent by putting your family and kids as first priority; never compromise the value of your home.
- Christie Berteau[24]

Forty-four percent of P.K.'s interviewed said they did feel at some point that they came second to the ministry.[25]

To effectively strategize and create boundaries, identify your enemies, especially those that frequently invade your territory. I refer to the telephone as "The Great Beast," and the day our ministry family decided to disconnect it, was the day our family time honestly became quality time spent together. Cell phones make this particularly tough, as they so easily become an extension of one's head.

A cell phone commercial once depicted men and women walking into the doctor's office with their head tilted to the side and their hand held up to their ear as if they had a disease. As humorous as it appears, it's an accurate portrayal of many people who seem addicted to the phone.

Home or Second Office?

By nature, ministry individuals are talkers, and if you're not careful, the telephone can become another branch of your ministry. This could result in making your home a second office. I understand the value and the need for a pastor to be able to be reached during times of emergency. There are systems where an emergency pager or "pastor on call" cell phone can be passed around on a pastoral team. An answering service to contact a pastor during times of need is very understandable, even needed. The point is, however, that we need to take charge of the "great beast," so that it does not take charge of our families.

Author Tim Elmore writes in his book, *Nurturing the Leader Within Your Child*[26], that the focus should remain on the quality of time you spend with them, not just the quantity. You could be home seven nights a week, but if your kids are in the backyard playing hide and seek, and you're frequently discussing your next business meeting as you sit in the kitchen, you're hardly spending quality time with your family.

Slaying the "Great Beast"

As soon as you resolve to limit or eliminate taking work calls at home, I promise that inevitably the phone will ring in the middle of a serious conversation or right when you sit down to a family dinner. These moments could be described as "the great beast rearing its ugly head." In the heat of the battle for our attention, my parents would get up and disconnect it, and each small victory drew us closer together as a family.

Before you begin the rationalization of why you need to keep your home phone or cell phone on, and how detrimental it would be if the outside world could not contact you, relax and remind yourself your children need you to be a parent and not just a provider. When you disconnect the phone, don't do it discreetly, especially when your children are small. Vocalize what you are doing, so they begin to understand the importance of the act, as well as their importance to you. In every instance, my brother and I slowly grew more confident that we took priority over the ministry, and the foundation of love and trust only grew stronger. To this day, we don't even have an answering machine.

Undivided Attention to Home

Between e-mails, cell phones and your voice mail at work, whatever needs to be taken care of will be waiting for you at the office. It's important to hear the church's needs, but ministry cannot be your total life. Remind yourself that you are a parent first. If you gain the whole world but lose your own children, you have lost everything. Place your full attention and full energy toward the ministry while you're at the office, being efficient with your time, and then when you come home – be all there… even if it means disconnecting the "Great Beast."

Principle #3: Focus on the quality of time you spend with your children more than the quantity of time.

Loving Boundary #4 – Make your retreat their retreat

Raising children is a creative endeavor, an art rather than a science. – Bruno Betterhein[27]

As a minister, there will always be times when you have to be out of town, but by making your retreat a retreat for them too, you not only guard them but also add excitement to their lives. This is one way parenting can truly become a creative art rather than a duty. Most parents don't enjoy going away from their children, and they work hard to ensure their kids don't feel like they're being left behind. How do you make them feel positive about your being away and keep them from feeling like they are being left behind? Make your "retreat" also be their retreat.

The minute my parents knew the dates of when they would be out of town, they began planning what became "our retreat," a week of fun designed entirely by my brother and myself. As a family we sat down, took out a calendar, and told our parents whom we most wanted to spend time with while they were gone. It never felt like they were lining up baby-sitters, because they honestly scheduled a week packed with fun activities that we normally didn't get a chance to do. Your kids' excitement will grow as they anticipate spending time with their best friends, going to their favorite places, and planning it all by themselves. Once our week had been planned, we placed the calendar on the refrigerator and began counting down the days.

The most important thing a father can do for his children is to love their mother. - Theodore Hesburght[28]

The plan worked brilliantly every time. This especially went well when it came time for their anniversary "honeymoon" trip. By doing this, they made time for themselves and still made sure their kids didn't feel like they were getting the raw end of the deal.

Principle #4: Traveling can be a win-win situation if you approach it the right way.

Loving Boundary #5 – Prioritize family time in your budget.
Dear Pastor, as a P.K., if I could tell you one thing…

Make time at home fun for your kids, and they will laugh about their "family fun" for years. - Jonathan Piersall[29]

Going on vacations, eating out at restaurants, enjoying amusement parks all have one thing in common–they require money. It's not uncommon for most people to spend three to four dollars a day at a local Starbuck's or spend thirty dollars a week on fast food, but as all financial planners will tell you, cutting back on the little things leads to big dividends. Saving is not always easy, but it is far less difficult when you're saving with a purpose.

Why is it important to budget money specifically for family time? It isn't because your kids want month-long European vacations, but they do want lifelong memories. What makes a family special? It's the traditions you create that wind up being the stories they tell for years to come. Thursday night pizza and games; station wagon trips to Baskin Robbins every Sunday after church; camping trips every summer (that always wind up in a disaster)–those are the priceless family moments. Remember the scripture that tells us where your treasure is, there your heart will be also? Where is your treasure?

Memory-Making... Priceless

My parents began to consciously sacrifice small things so that they could create weekly, monthly, and annual traditions, and I am confident they haven't regretted it for a second. There are a million ways to do this in your home, but it starts with you and your spouse taking the first step. Open up your budget and take a look at where your money goes. You'll likely be very surprised. Trim expenses that are not necessities to make room in your budget for family fun.

Get the whole family into the act in preparing for that trip to Six Flags or Disney World. Set jars around the house to collect spare change. Maybe everyone pitches in with some of their birthday money in the "Future Fun Bank," etc. Small actions like this can pay big dividends.

Your attitude and approach to your finances affects your children's attitudes as well, so make sure that fun and family time are both feasible and attainable. Don't stop at "We can't afford to do this, or we can't afford to go there." If you do this, your kids will not only feel sad, but also will feel helpless or victimized by their circumstances and begin to wonder why you're not paid more. Eventually this can lead to resentment. Make the little sacrifices now for the big payoff in fun family time a few months down the road.

Principle #5: Make sure your budget reflects family time as a priority and a goal.

Loving Boundary #6 – Make visible signs as a declaration.
Dear Pastor, as a P.K., if I could tell you one thing…

Please spend time with your kids, because even if they act like it doesn't matter, it means the world to them. - Anonymous P.K.

Even after doing all you know to do to give your kids your full attention, there will be times when people still come knocking at your door. A final boundary line you can draw, to seal your determined efforts, is to make signs for your front door. Not wanting to offend others, but also wanting to include us in this activity, my parents helped my brother and I make our own front-door signs.

When it came time for the four key nights a week when we were home as a family, on our door hung signs that said, "We're sorry, but tonight is family night." Other times it said, "Mom and dad are spending time with Justin and Josh right now." Yes, we really did make these signs, and we placed them on our front doors! To our amazement, they warded off countless family-time intruders and made us feel extremely special.

If a real emergency came up such as a tragic accident with someone in the church, the signs were friendly enough so that someone could still feel comfortable to interrupt. The point is not to "use" your kids to get away from ministry but to minister to your kids first. If a real issue comes up, it can still be dealt with. During those serious moments your children will perceive ministry to others in their time of need as a Christian virtue as well.

Seeing, hearing, experiencing: The Keys to Understanding

Before children understand anything, they must first see it, hear it, or experience it. If they are able to do all three, you've accomplished a huge task. As a man or woman in ministry, there are too many lines that can be crossed and blurred by the lifestyle you're living and the expectations of those to whom you minister. You must establish boundaries. Establish boundaries for the members of your church and your children to see. Everyone then knows where they clearly stand, and your kids can feel safe knowing they stand closest to you.

Principle #6: Manage the expectations of those to whom you minister…family and church.

When people approach my parents and other ministers whose children are living wholeheartedly for the Lord, they always want to know how to raise their children successfully in the context of ministry. I don't doubt for a second their hearts are any different from my parents' or other great parents'; the only difference is their strategic approach towards the issue of raising children.

One good action is worth a thousand good intentions.

One pastor's son described it as his parents being *very deliberate* in how they raised him and his four siblings. It isn't enough just to want the best; you must also take steps towards establishing an environment that makes it all possible. John Mason says, "One good action is worth a thousand good intentions."[30] Your kids want your right intentions, but ultimately they're dependent upon your right actions.

THINK ABOUT IT...

Considering that "one good action is worth a thousand good intentions," and as you reflect on the loving boundaries our family created, write down some loving boundaries that could move some of your good intentions into actions. Remember, drawing loving boundaries now prevents us from drawing battle lines later.

Reflect on the boundaries:

#1 – Be at home more often than you are away.

How many nights a week will you and your spouse allow yourselves to be gone?

#2 – Make big events a big deal.

Write in all big events coming up in your calendar as appointments. Discuss with your spouse how you can make these events more special.

#3 – Disconnect the telephone.

Consider doing away with the answering machine, or turning off your phone's ringer during specific hours.

#4 – Make your retreat their retreat.

When is the next time you and your spouse will be gone? Begin planning their retreat.

#5 – Prioritize family time in your budget.

What areas can you cut back on financially to begin to save for a planned future family time?

#6 – Make the signs.

Sit down with your spouse and kids on the next family night and create signs for your door. Do them by hand or use a computer to graphically design them.

One of my favorite vacations: skiing

Another favorite vacation moment

**A school project I did one family night…
I ended up winning third place in a harvest contest
at school with this masterpiece**

Always made our games even if it was just t-ball

CHAPTER 5

The Chapter Parent's Can't Afford To Violate

My dad traveled consistently my whole life. I remember crying every time he left. - Anonymous P.K.

As time went on, dad spent less time with the family and more time with the ministry. - Anonymous P.K.

Most rules are easy to live by when it's convenient, but due to the nature of ministry, the opportunity to compromise will come disguised in the form of ministry success. When the inevitable change of circumstances comes, your commitments cannot be conditional. Even if you "become famous" in ministry, your highest priority must always be your position at home. My parents remained my heroes long after they began receiving invitations to speak all over the country, because they continued to make my brother and me a priority in their lives even when it became more difficult to do so.

As your ministry grows and the speaking opportunities increase, remember that no amount of money or fame replaces your presence in your home. Above all, remain consistent in the boundaries you set, especially in this area of future opportunity, but also in the privacy of your home.

Maintain balance in ministry and family.

There is a definite balance needed between allowing God to use you in ministry and still being significant to your children. As I previously mentioned, my parents stayed committed to this rule – to only allow themselves to do outside ministry two days per month. My father, as senior pastor, spoke very little outside our area, because he wanted to make sure his flock was being cared for, but both he and mom had numerous invitations. Yet for twenty years, until my brother and I were out of the house, they adhered to this rule tenaciously.

Other ministers incur unusual circumstances and need to find their own rules to stand by. One anonymous ministry worker whose grandfather died and left behind a large ministry said her parents had to work things out to keep the ministry going. "When my grandfather died, my parents inherited a lot more responsibilities, but when it came to ministering far away, they made sure at least one of them was home with us. We heard them often say they were committed to raising us themselves, not allowing someone else to do it."

In Song of Solomon 1:6, the Lord gives pastors a verse to remember: "They made me the keeper of the vineyards, but my own vineyard I have not kept."[31] As you keep and maintain the vineyards of others, always make sure you're taking care of your own.

Glamorous or Significant?

Dear Pastor, as a P.K., if I could tell you one thing…

You're not pastors who have kids, you are parents who are pastors. Be the exact same person at home as you are at the church…just be normal. - Joy Delgatty[32]

As the doors to fame begin to open, I believe the most important question you can ask yourself is—am I doing this because it is glamorous or significant?

Opportunities can be beneficial to your reputation but detrimental to your family. Most men and women who have admired my parents often have wondered why they gave up so many speaking engagements, but truthfully the reason was always found in their priorities. They knew that while having their name in brochures and on billboards may be glamorous, it was not as significant as their role as parents or as pastors.

It may not always feel as glamorous to go home and take care of your family instead of having thousands listen to you preach, but in the end, it may be the most needed ministry you give.

Your children - living clay - and the full-time heart

Your primary ministry is to mold and shape the "living clay" that sleeps under your roof and carries your last name. The clay you've been called to mold requires your full-time heart. You cannot simply coast once they're old enough to be on their own. Every moment to mold significance into their lives can quickly be replaced with the opportunity for you to cultivate glamour. Once those significant moments pass, they cannot be regained. As parents, you alone hold the final responsibility for the clay that's been placed in your hands.

> *I took a piece of plastic clay*
> *And idly fashioned it one day,*
> *And as my fingers pressed it still,*
> *It moved and yielded to my will.*
> *I came again when days were passed*
> *The bit of clay was hard at last;*
> *The form I gave it, it still bore,*
> *But I could change that form no more.*

I took a piece of living clay
And gently formed it day by day,
And molded with my power and art
A young child's soft and yielding heart,
I came again when years were gone
It was a man I looked upon;
He still that early impress wore,
And I could change him nevermore. [33]

While growing up, I remember hearing my dad call out our names in prayer every morning. -Ruth (Daugherty) Sanders[34]

How often are you praying for your kids? Set a specific time aside each day.

Does the grass grow on your path?

Prayer holds a definite priority in the preparation of your children, but it is not a seasonal discipline. Prayer is a lifestyle. History tells us that early African Christian converts earnestly and regularly took time in private devotions. Each man and woman had a designated path in the thickets of the fields where they would pour out their hearts to God. Over time, these paths became quite worn, and by walking past, one would immediately know that the well-trodden paths reflected a solid prayer life. However, the ones who struggled in their prayer lives were kindly reminded, "Brother, the grass grows on your path."

I would like to take a moment in this book to ask you a very important question: Where is your private spot of prayer? It is vitally important not to allow the "grass to grow" in your prayer closet. Neglect in this area presents great danger. Don't let even one day pass that you don't bless your church, your staff, even your food, nor should a day pass that you are not specifically lifting up your kids in prayer.

This is not a drill … it's the real thing.

This whole parenting thing is not a rough draft or a test-run. The mistakes are costly. This sobering reality should not cause you to give up hope, but to increase your conscious decision to pray daily for the amazing family God's entrusted in your care. You need to pray. There is no greater key to significant parenting in the ministry than prayer, and I promise you that even though your children might take it for granted at times, they will never forget it.

Mary, Queen of Scotland, was once quoted as saying, "I fear John Knox's prayers more than an army of ten thousand men."[35] May hell fear your prayers and be defeated by your faithfulness in consistent intercession. Draw your boundaries and refuse to make exceptions, both publicly and privately.

THINK ABOUT IT…

1. What are some ministry opportunities that look glamorous to you right now? Carefully consider a plan to balance how you will allow God to use you in that ministry opportunity while you also reserve enough time and emotional energy to still bring significant worth to your family. What is that plan?

2. When it comes to raising kids, prayer is a must! Here are some questions you may want to frequently ask yourself: "How often am I praying for my kids?" "Am I modeling prayer to my children, and would they know where my private spot of prayer is?" "What am I teaching my family about prayer?"

3. Whether a spouse, staff member or a close friend, do you currently have someone who can motivate you to pray and who can speak candidly to you about your prayer times? If not, find someone who will gently remind you, "Friend, the grass grows on your path."

My favorite picture of Dad praying featured in the local newspaper…Dad, thank you for your example

CHAPTER 6

Everyday Life-Defining Moments

Straight from the hearts of P.K.'s: When asked about entering the ministry, 17% were negative, 78% were positive, 5% were undecided.[36]

"A group of elderly, cultured gentlemen met often to exchange wisdom and drink tea. Each host tried to find the finest and most costly varieties, to create exotic blends that would arouse the admiration of his guests.

When the most venerable and respected of the group entertained, he served his tea with unprecedented ceremony, measuring the leaves from a golden box. The assembled conosures praised this exquisite tea. The host smiled and said, 'The tea you have found so delightful is the same tea our peasants drink. I hope it will be a reminder to all that the good things in life are not necessarily the rarest or the most costly.'"[37]

Often parents think that the rarest and most costly gifts are the ones that they need to provide for their children. We all want to give our kids great memories and any great parent would try to give their children the world if it were at all possible. Sometimes we can get caught up in pouring our efforts into the Disney Land vacations and the dream-come-true Christmas presents. Even as parents, we are looking for the "perfect tea." While the big moments that my parents gave me were meaningful, the life-defining moments that they created for me were found in the normal everyday. Let me give you just a couple ideas to make your everyday moments with your child life defining.

Your kids must win in the battle for your time and attention.

My dad ALWAYS kept an open door policy with us kids. No matter how important the meeting, we could always see him or call him. - Kellie (Berteau) Williams[38]

One simple truth that has solidified my relationship with my parents and my relationship with the Lord is the knowledge that "I win." I'm not insinuating that I'm competing with anyone or anything; it's just that never for a second have I questioned where I stood with my parents. I'm sure all parents feel this way about their kids and want their children to know this, but to do what it takes to reinforce this in the minds of their kids is a whole other story.

One key rule that my parents set in place was that Justin and I reserved the right to interrupt anything at any moment, even to just say "Hi," or "I love you." It wouldn't have made a difference if they were talking to the President or Rev. Billy Graham, we would win a moment of their time.

Now, I realize that there has to be a correct balance to this rule, but rarely will your children take advantage of these rules in a negative way. They will recognize when it is inappropriate to interrupt. Family and ministry are on different levels of priority. Showing your son or daughter their importance in your priorities means more to your children than you will ever realize. Once they fully understand this, they won't push the boundaries.

Truthfully, you will want them to exercise this right far more often than they will. Most kids only interrupt when they need money or want you to do something for them, but your response to these interruptions will determine how often they stop in to see you when it really matters.

Communication is the key to solid family relationships.

Communication is vital to any relationship – family, friend, or marriage. No conversation is insignificant. A child may need your attention in conversation as much as the teenager or adult. Pay attention to the "just stopped by to say hi" moments, for you will find that your children have far more to say than just "hi."

Trust me, speaking as a former child, a teenager, and now as a young adult, there is usually a reason I "stop in" to see my mom or dad whether I like to admit it or not. I may not need an hour of their time, but there are moments I may need my parents between the hours of 8 a.m. and 6 p.m.

If I stop in at a bad time or in the middle of a serious appoint-ment, they always assure me that they want to talk to me, and then they ask me if I can stick around for a few minutes. At other times they might take the hint and offer to take me out to lunch. Let me clearly state that I didn't walk in with a sign on my forehead that said, "Help! I'm hurting, and I need your support," nor will your chil-dren, but a wise parent will sense that.

As P.K.'s, we tell ourselves that you as ministers deal with enough problems, and we don't want to add to your load. We attempt to hide it, because we only want you to listen if you want to. Our bait is the "just saying hi" test. I beg you to be an attentive parent who looks and listens when your child stops by. You will often find out what's really going on inside your child's head.

Cultivating Open, Caring Communication

The principle of assuring your children, so they know that they win in your eyes, will earn you the key moments you've been waiting for—the times where they open up and tell you how they really feel.

As you establish an open-door policy, you show your children that it doesn't matter how insignificant the issue is ... you want to hear about it. The thought that you're too busy or don't want to be interrupted will no longer exist. As they grow older and the issues they deal with become more complicated, you'll have erased their fear of coming to you when something serious does occur. Above all I want you to know that when you, as our parents, let us win, you win more than just our confidence and our respect; you win our hearts.

Timing is everything.
Dear Pastor, as a P.K., if I could tell you one thing...

Remember, your job as a parent is not to reproduce yourself in your children, but to reproduce Christ. - Jason McCutchen[39]

Once you've set an open-door policy in motion, you'll need to get comfortable with flexibility. Talking when children want to talk isn't easy, but if you want the lines to stay open and frequent, it's unavoidable. The first step in communicating is always listening, and this requires you to be available on their timetable.

Many of the significant talks I've had with my parents came at the most random times, and those talks ended up impacting my life in more ways than I thought possible. With kids, especially teenagers (if you have them, you've already discovered this), their most open moments will come late at night. Teenagers deal with many different thoughts and emotions when they drive home after being out with their friends or a boyfriend or girlfriend.

Extra-Mile Availability
At those times, be especially available to your children as their parent and as their friend. Don't interrogate at these times, but do feel free to ask open-ended questions to get the ball rolling. A possible question might be something like, "I know you'll say you're

fine and everything is good, but tell me honestly … what can I do to be a better friend and parent for you?" Even just a simple, "Is there something bothering you that you want to talk about?" will start the flow of conversation in a comfortable way.

Cautiously make sure they know you're not there to interrogate them, but as their parent and friend you just want to know about their life. After awhile you will begin to notice a pattern. In my house, growing up, it typically went like this:

Justin would walk in and take off his shoes to head up the stairs to his room. Occasionally, one or both of my parents would intentionally sleep out on the couches. Even though they appeared to be sleeping, Justin would lean over and say quietly, "Hey Mom – How was your day?" My mom or dad's head would pop up, they'd get up off the couch and walk towards the stairs and prepare to listen. For hours mom or dad would position themselves on the floor, occasionally asking questions early into the morning hours to show their concern.

It's hard to say how often this happened or how many times the conversations were focused solely on where we'd been or how much fun we'd had. But without a doubt when questions arose about girls, relationships, fears, and future plans, we always initiated those conversations when we were ready. A wise parent knows their children will talk on their own time.

Parents who know their children will keep themselves ready and available for when those special sharing moments arise. These moments are your opportunity to pour your wisdom and experience into your child's life while helping your child to develop their decision-making abilities and lifestyle.

Dear pastor, as a P.K., if I could tell you one thing…

Never tell your kids to do something and then when they ask 'Why?' don't say, 'Because I told you so.' Explain to them why, talk about your regrets in life, and teach them to avoid those wrong decisions and why. - Anonymous P.K.

A 24-Hour-a-day Job

From the day you watched your son or daughter come into the world, you became their first mentor and teacher, the first one to exemplify Jesus to them. What an exciting and overwhelming privilege and calling this is. And, what an adventure! You can expect this to be a roller coaster ride like nothing you've ever experienced, full of ups and downs, thrills, and stomach-plummeting moments.

In spite of the heroes built up by society, from movie stars to superhuman characters, statistics say nearly forty percent of all American teenagers want to be like their parents. Believe it or not, your children will look to emulate your life, not what they see on a movie screen or in magazines, because you being their hero and mentor is not just something they need; it's something they want.

Last Words ... and First Words

Your key moments to develop your children almost always occur after hours, those evening times when they come home from school, after a game, right before curfew on a Friday night. Whose voice do you want your kids to hear at the end of the day?

Deep down, most parents really want to have the last word about most circumstances their kids will go through, and trust me, as teenagers, we may appear not to care, but we respect your opinion. We realize that you are usually correct in your assessment of most situations from the wisdom of experience you have gained. Let me give you a principle from the "other side of the chair." To earn the last word in the hearts and minds of your children, you must allow them to have the first word.

One night my brother, who wasn't living at home, called late at night. I knew my already-sleeping dad had a sermon to preach the next morning and had been sick all week. But I woke him anyway. He stumbled out of his room and I watched as he lay on the floor with the phone in hand. Nearly an hour later I came upstairs and he was still there, just listening. Suddenly I realized all the times I too had called home late at night, it never occurred to me he might be sick or tired or have a sermon to prepare. He sacrificed it all knowing that if he would listen, eventually we would too.

- Anonymous P.K.

Teach them to fish...

Raising self-sufficient children in the ministry accurately reflects the old proverb of the man who took his son to fish, for he knew that if he caught a fish, he would only feed his son for a day. But if he taught his son to fish, his son would be fed for a lifetime.

Begin to trust that God orders their steps, as you begin to teach them how to walk– developing in them the strong habits of daily prayer, time in the Word, and solid decision-making abilities. By instilling in me these habits, my parents were teaching me how to fish by daily modeling it before my eyes. On numerous occasions, I walked into my dad's study only to find him praying or reading his Bible. Your behind-the-scenes relationship with God carries far more weight with your children than your words from the pulpit. I watched my parents' consistency and faithfulness to be godly indi-viduals, and that led to a life I began to emulate. Your children will do the same.

We, as your children, take great solace in knowing your ministry is not an occupation you turn on and off, but a lifestyle that influ-ences every minute of your day. In order to raise children who love God, please emphasize your desire for them to live with full-time hearts regardless of whether they enter the ministry. Teach them by your lifestyle, and help them see that the joy and desire of ministry are what propel you to do what you do and live the way you live.

Passion for Christ is contagious.

Most couples who are happily married make those around them desire strong relationships as well. Anyone watching admires them for their relationship, yet may have questions about how it happened, how they maintain it, and how they deal with difficult circumstances. In much the same way, let the core of your life as a minister be built around that which is most important, which is your relationship with Christ. Allow their questions and make your love affair with Jesus be so attractive they can't help but desire it.

The decision of whether or not to enter full-time ministry inevitably is up to them, but once their hearts and lives are committed to Jesus, you can proudly know that you've raised children who will hear God's voice clearly.

Supernatural, Life-Defining Moments

My dad was also my buddy...he often took me out on dates as a little girl. - Anonymous P.K., Female

Without our traditions, we would be as shaky as the fiddler on the roof. -Tevye[40]

Some of my most remembered, most treasured, and most learned-from moments came during all the less-than-glamorous lunch appointments. From pizzas to turkey croissant sandwiches with yellow mustard, there's something quite special about one-on-one time at a restaurant with your parent. Maybe it's their undivided attention, maybe it's the treat of eating out with a good excuse but going out to lunch or on a date with a parent holds great meaning for any child.

It's from these designated appointment times that the questions about life, ministry, and relationships emerge. During times like these I was able to truly share what was going on inside my life. These times did more than create a good memory. They were times where I gained love, wisdom, and advice that saved me from countless "could be" disasters. Grabbing a sandwich, ordering a pizza, heading out for ice cream all served one purpose, to get us to talk so that we might become closer friends. It worked. Today there are far fewer mentoring moments I can recall outside of our favorite restaurants. *Find a day when you can take your kids out to lunch. Make a bakery, a coffee shop, or a pizzeria a place they'll never forget.*

Training Through Your Experiences

Dear Pastor, as a P.K., if I could tell you one thing …

It's all a learning experience. My dad often sat me down and talked to me about something I'd done. He would go on to explain what other kids do, what he went through, and then the consequences to the actions. - Marcus Haggard[41]

My parents always sat down with me and talked with me…they were always teaching. - R.J. Tate[42]

My parents both lead hectic lives. They always have. Once in a while when Justin or I needed to talk with one of them or when we had questions, our moments with our parents became what I liked to call, "Walk with me?" moments. On the way to an appointment, we'd approach mom about something, and she'd respond with a sincere desire to listen but say something like, "Tell me about it. Come, walk with me." It was during these times that Justin and I found another moment to talk with our parents.

Sometimes my parents even used these moments to tell us about what was going on in their lives or what struggles they were facing. We gained priceless wisdom and expertise just by being a listening ear during these brief talks, and during our talks we would gain strength from each other as family members.

I remember hearing my mom say, "Josh the only comfort I get out of this trial I'm enduring is in knowing that you can watch and learn from what I'm facing, because I know one day you'll go through something similar." Consider it a unique privilege that as you walk through hard times, your children can learn from your experiences without holding the responsibility of the consequences. Developing them through your own experiences must be a conscious decision you make.

It can become far too easy to vent at the supper table about what's going on at the church or with the ministry. Therefore, choose your words carefully; deliberately involve your children and direct comments towards them as you turn your "pain into purpose." As the primary example to your children, remember that after awhile they'll begin to not only verbally respond to situations in ways that you have, but by the grace of God they will live out the same principles you've taught them during these moments.

A Keepsake Chest

When Justin and I were younger, our parents purchased a keepsake chest for each of us. It served two purposes: To help rid dad and mom of items they no longer had room for, and to provide us with a way to hold on to childhood memorabilia. Safely stored in my chest are my first baseball uniform, my high school graduation gown, treasured baseball cards, and a plaster cast of my hand print when I was seven. These are just a few of the things in my nostalgic collection.

It seems the older people get, the more they tend to save everything. I don't know that I am an advocate of saving every single elementary school assignment, every single photograph, and every single toy ever used. I do know that by saving significant things and by becoming a "memory-oriented" person, this will help me create a sense of appreciation for the small things that could otherwise be so easily overlooked. In the Old Testament, the people of Israel built altars, which served as a tangible reminder of a specific event or moment in their lives. Every time the younger Israelites walked past a small pile of rocks, the older generation would tell the story of "The time when...". We live in a fast-paced society, surrounded by an unappeased, ungrateful, and unimpressed populace. Teach your children the joy of remembering, the value of memories, and cultivate in them the ability to discover God's faithfulness and goodness day to day. Make a conscious effort to be the ones turning their eyes to God, because everything else will attempt to turn their eyes away from Him!

All parents need parenting models.

As pastors, we often recognize the need to model our churches, our ministries, and our lives as ministers after others who are farther up the ministry mountain. We must do the same with our families. We all need parenting models.

A favorite quote of mine is, "The years will teach you what the days will never know."[43] My parents believed that one of the best ways to become better is to learn from those who've lived through years of experience—especially those in ministry who have children. In my opinion, they're right.

Finding Your Parenting Model

How do you find someone after which to model your parenting style? Seek them out. Look for someone else in ministry who has raised their children successfully and who seems to be wise, as well as approachable. Express your admiration for their family, and present your request humbly and sincerely. Let them know you'd like to set aside one night a month to have them over for dinner or meet them for coffee and then let the questions fly.

Established times of "parenting-in-the-ministry" mentoring can provide you with countless insights and answers. And as an added benefit, you might even create a great friendship.

THINK ABOUT IT...

1. Do you currently have a parenting model? If not, work on finding your parenting model by seeking out a couple in ministry who you've watched raise children successfully and seem to be wise as well as approachable. Express your admiration for their family, and present your request humbly and sincerely. Let them know you'd like to set aside some time to have them over for dinner or meet them for coffee, and then let the questions fly. Write out some questions you would like to ask them.

2. There will be times where your children may open up and tell you how they really feel, but most of the time it is masked in the everyday "just saying hi" test they give you. Are you willing to set aside your schedule to stop long enough to hear what is NOT being said? Write down some ways to help you foster open and honest communication with your kids. How will you communicate to your children that THEY "WIN" in your eyes?

Here were some of the chapter ideas:
   1) Create an open-door policy.
   2) Know when your child is most likely to open up, and be sure to make yourself available at those times even if it is after their curfew.
   3) Take them on "dates."
   4) Don't always try to have the "last word."
   5) Ask questions such as, "How can I honestly be a better friend and parent to you?"

**Always there for me in life-defining moments like prom,
homecoming and soccer championship games (What I
remember most were sharing these moments with Mom and
Dad and being able to talk about them later on)**

CHAPTER 7

Friendships: The Make-It Or Break-It Factor

Whether we want to believe it or not, statistics tell us that your child's actions and beliefs are highly influenced by their peer groups. In many cases it is said that your child is more influenced on a daily basis by their friends than by you, their parents. Your child's friends can either be your greatest asset or your worst enemy. My parents chose to make them one of their greatest assets.

I learned very early the importance of the people I spent most of my time with. My parents would tell us, "Your friends are like the buttons on an elevator. They either take you UP or they take your DOWN." Just as Proverbs 13:20 tells us, "Whoever walks with the wise will grow wise; whoever walks with fools will suffer harm."[44] My mom and I both often say, "Show me your friends, and I'll show you your future."

Still, my parents did more than just tell us the importance of grooming good friendships; they consistently went the extra mile to make sure that our house was one of my friends' favorite places to hang out. When we were in elementary school, my folks let us dig a massive hole (a pit actually) in our backyard in our sincere determination to build an "underground hideout." When we became teenagers, they let us put all the furniture out on the front lawn so we could set up a large trampoline indoors, and right in the middle of our living room no less! In short, they did everything possible to make it easy for people to want to be our friends.

Dear Pastor, as a P.K., if I could tell you one thing..

Help keep your children accountable and on track by staying informed as to what's going on in their lives and who they are hanging out with. Their friends will be a big key to what is really going on in their lives. - Daniel Macintosh, P.K.[45]

The importance of building friends must not be overlooked.

The importance of your child's friendships must never be overlooked, and the reasons are varied. The foremost reason is that many parents innocently believe that as long as their children are attending church and/or spending their time in a Christian environment that they'll be making lifelong, godly friends (or at least "acceptable" ones). This is not always the case. Your child's friendship development will take effort and must be carefully guarded even if their friendships are being built at church or in a Christian environment.

Churches, if they are any good, will always reach out to a lost and dying world. Likewise, Christian parents, if they are doing their job, will "drag" their family to church. What I am saying is basic. Look around the church and there will probably be numerous non-believing, "not so perfect" teenagers who are forced to attend by their parents. These "outreach opportunities" may even be the children of your most faithful church volunteers, which only increases the potential time your child may spend with them. Without going overboard and placing your child in a "bubble," the point here is simple: please don't overlook the importance of the "right kind of friends" for your child. Yes, they may have friends within the four walls of the church, but what kind of friends are they?

It is at this point where you need to understand that helping your child choose the right friends may not be as easy as asking them if their new friend goes to church. Your active role in helping them to find the right friends should make you very aware of what they are choosing to do when they hang out with their friends, even if they are "church friends." There is a phrase I believe applies here, "We can have Christian friends, but many of us do not have friendships that are Christian." Maybe you need to change your question from, "Are they with Christian/church friends?" to "Are their friends encouraging them toward Christian living?" which is the key. In addition to these previous thoughts and consistent fervent prayer, let me tell you a few ways I believe you can encourage your children to create friendships that will go the distance.

Idea #1 — Create the atmosphere.

I am blown away by the amount of advertising money that restaurants and businesses spend to attract a person to do business with them. Companies drop thousands to millions of dollars to attract and keep their customers. The logic is that if the customer isn't spending their time and money there, they are doing it somewhere else. They are intentional on creating an atmosphere that will attract and keep their customers. You should be as well. I'm not implying that millions (or even thousands) should be spent to keep your kids and their friends around the house, but I do want you to consider your home atmosphere.

One of the greatest "atmosphere" decisions my parents made was to invest in some items that made my house the one where my friends wanted to spend time. My brother and I honestly had it really good. Our basement was filled with many exciting things that were purchased throughout the years to keep my friends and me busy: a ping-pong table, bumper pool, a large air hockey table (actually two at one point), a small wall basketball hoop, a basketball court outside, and a great lounging area with a 100=CD jukebox. My friends and I were surrounded with great "What do you want to do tonight?" options. All this was an attempt to create an atmosphere that begged us to spend our time at home. My parents clearly understood that creating a great atmosphere at the house allowed them to know what we were doing and with whom.

Idea #2 — Hold your own party.

One area that many parents in Christian ministry seem to either ignore or just don't believe is possible, is that their "perfect" child could be involved in "partying." The reason for going to these parties is simple: friends. You go for the friends and then you do stupid things while you are there to gain attention from your friends. My parents understood the magnetism that these events held and the problems they could create. Instead of fighting them...they blew them away.

Did my parents really let us party??? Yes, they allowed us to hold our own parties – at our house with them around. Not only were they continuing to help create and control the right atmosphere as I just previously mentioned, but they also helped to address future questionable places where we may have looked to create friends. Some of these parties included Thanksgiving dinners with 100 of our friends attending (our friends brought most of the food and desserts). Another was a costume party that my whole senior class attended. It was a blast watching all my friends "walk the runway" in their costumes. The first-place costume winner received a hundred dollars that my parents dished out. Then you can't forget our Frozen Turkey Basketball Tournament, our Christmas parties, and the many others that my parents helped us host to make sure that we were making the right kind of friends in an atmosphere that reinforced what we as a family believed. These parties were not only a great idea, but in time they helped my brother find a venue for reaching out to some of his unsaved friends that he had been trying to reach.

Without going into all of the details, my brother, with the help of my mother, planned what would become known as "Matthew Parties." Taken from the idea in scripture where Matthew would invite his unsaved friends to a "party" to get them around Jesus, my brother would invite hundreds...yes hundreds of students to these parties. Then my brother and mom would saturate the party with a ton of fun Christians making sure that the Christians were the majority at the party. The object of the night was to give non-Christians a chance to be around Jesus by having a lot of fun and getting invited to a youth service by a sharp and fun Christian. My brother and friends didn't preach; they just created an atmosphere and then built relationships so that Jesus could later be experienced. Let's just say the idea went over very well. Without exaggeration, hundreds of people came. As these "outreach parties" continued through the years, we eventually had to move them out of our house and rent a local community hall. I guess that's what happens when your "Matthew parties" begin having upwards of 800 people in attendance.

Idea #3 — Continue to "fan" their correct friendship decisions.

When we address our child's negative friendship choices, it many times may feel (from your child's perspective) that you are personally attacking them. One idea I would like to reinforce is that of focusing on their right friendship choices. I am not suggesting that you ignore the wrong ones (many times they definitely need to be addressed), but I am suggesting that you place even greater attention on any correct decisions that they are making in the friendship arena. I realize that we all understand this concept, but the problem many times still painfully remains. Even with well-meaning intentions, many times all your child may hear is the "noise" you are making over their incorrect decisions.

Kent Kjellstrom, Ryan Minnick, and Adam Haugen were just a few friends that my parents continued to applaud. I remember the day that my mother began subtly reminding me how Kent was such a great friend to me. She would point out areas in which he really supported me. In doing so, she just reinforced in my mind the value of his friendship. She was trying to strategically fan and applaud the correct friendship choice I was making. Significant friends are few and far between, and my parents made sure that they encouraged potential friendships that could leave a positive impact on me.

The simple phrase, "what gets rewarded gets repeated" comes to mind, and it works both ways. When your child makes friendship decisions that are "made of the right stuff"…let your child know. Even if it's an old friendship, give praise to past positive decisions they have made with your words of affirmation. Whether your child admits it or not, how you feel about the decisions that are made makes a huge impact on the future direction that is taken.

When you see friends in your child's life that you know would be a strong influence or support to them, take the initiative to encourage those relationships. Invite them over or have them go out to eat with your family. Invest in their activities. Pay for a Christian concert or other positive activities that they may enjoy together. Simply put, do all that you can to foster their positive peer relationships without crossing the lines of being controlling or too overbearing.

Idea #4 — "The Why Behind the What" – An Act of Coaching

Coaching involves not only the process of helping a person know what to do, but it's also helping them understand why they want to do it and how it benefits them. I like to call this the "why behind the what." As I'm sure you already know, your child doesn't want to be told to do something — they want to come to their own conclusions. When we correctly coach our child, we help them come to their own conclusions about their friends.

Jewish culture believes that one of the best ways to coach or teach someone is through the process of asking questions. When a Jewish teacher is asked a question, the teacher responds by giving their answer in the form of a question. This then requires the student to give an answer. If the student is wise they will not respond by giving a direct answer — they will continue the process by wrapping their answer in an additional question for the teacher. This questioning process continues, allowing the student to truly learn what they believe and understand the "why" behind what the teacher is saying. Discernment concerning good and bad friendships will come when your child is able to arrive at their own conclusions of why certain friendships are right or wrong for them and not just because mom or dad told them so. Their personal evaluation of friendships, and the understanding of their right choices, makes a lot more sense to them when it can happen on their level. So, ask sincere questions about their friends that make them think about who they are spending time with.

Idea #5 — Strengthen your own friendship with them.

It could probably go without saying, especially in this book, but please continue to strengthen your own friendship with your child. Just because they are your son or daughter doesn't mean that they are also your friend. One of the greatest ways to help your kids pick good friends is for them to try to base it off of their friendship with you. And believe it or not, when your friendship with them is strong, their choice to measure new friendships by the one they have with you happens quite often. When their relationship with you is shaky, they usually look to others to strengthen that "lack of something" in their life. I like to say, "A hungry need is a dangerous need." If that hunger for a strong relationship with their mom and dad isn't correctly met at home, their need to get it met somewhere else will usually turn out to be a negative experience, nine times out of ten.

Moments will come when honest feedback has to be given in regards to their new friendship choices. When your relationship with them is strong, you have leverage to just say, "Hey, you're better than that! You can't be spending time with them — let's talk about why." As you follow some of the suggestions above and continue to strengthen your friendship with them, these moments can be handled with a lot more confidence and success!

A closing thought about relationships with the opposite sex ...

When it comes to relationships with the opposite sex...good luck! No, seriously though, friendship and dating relationship problems are similar enough that I didn't think I could end this chapter without at least briefly addressing it. Another entire book could be written on helping your child navigate this part of their life!

But, here are a few short thoughts:

- Look at the ideas given above. Many of the friendship principles can cross over into the dating world.

- Teach them what I call "Relationship Mathematics." Most people enter relationships looking for someone to "complete them." This is a huge mistake. My Relationship Mathematics states that two emotionally needy people, the kind who are looking to "be completed" by another's love, will never be able to form an emotionally whole relationship. Only two emotionally secure people can form a relationship that is complete.

- Teach them to never date someone who has the "potential" to be perfect for them. In other words, they should never start a relationship off the basis that the other person could be so incredible if they just changed a couple areas in their life or if someone just believed in them. Dating someone because you believe in what they *could be* instead of *who they are right now* has gotten many a teenager, and adult, into serious relationship trouble.

- Teach them to "give it the test of time." When looking at someone to date, they should pray and watch the person they'd like to date, giving any potential dating relationship the "test of time." If God is in it, with time it will come about. Giving the decision some serious "watching and praying" time has saved many from making a hasty mistake.

- Teach them that dating is a way to find a mate, not a form of social entertainment.

- Make a list with them early in their life of what they want and don't want in a mate. When the time(s) comes when they are considering dating someone, they'll have a list to go by. From that list they are then able to see if they are compromising on what they truly want in a mate or if this person could be the wonderful possibility that they have prayed for.

- Ask them the question: "What is your purpose?" If they can't answer that question, help show them that dating won't help them find their purpose. Already knowing their own true identity is key when it comes to dating.

Dating, just as any other significant relationship in life, will always make a huge impact on your child. As a good parent, strive to make inroads into your child's life now so that later when they are choosing who to be friends with and who to date, their closest friends resemble someone with your family values. Their spiritual heritage and family values should be what guides them in this adventure of life.

THINK ABOUT IT...

1. If the phrase, "We can have Christian friends, but many of us do not have friendships that are Christian," painfully makes too much sense when it comes to the friendships of your children, decide how you will begin to help them "shift gears." This shifting of gears really must happen first in their thoughts, so ask questions such as: "Do you like who you are when you hang out with _____?" "Do you think your speech or your actions change when you are with _____?" Write down some other questions unique to your situation that should be asked if this scenario hits home.

2. Write down a few of the people whom you believe to be the most influential friends in your kids' lives. How can you begin to positively influence these relationships? Pray for those friends today.

3. What are some dating guidelines you would like to set for your child? If you decide now, it will help when the time comes.

Best-friends

The best backyard treehouse ever

A huge costume party at our house

CHAPTER 8

Creating a Sense of Spiritual Heritage

For you have heard my vows, O God; you have given me the heritage of those who fear your name. Psalms 61:5[46]

Proud mothers, fathers, and relatives always tend to argue over whom a newborn baby most favors. Their little newborn is, without question, not only the most beautiful baby alive, but looks just like "his daddy" or "her mother." One minute he has his dad's eyes; the next minute you look at him and realize he has his mom's nose. After just a few short hours, the newborn's personality has already been decided for him or her, and the relatives conclude that the baby will be "just like" the mother or the father.

What's the point of the great debate? Why do family members find it so vital that the infant directly reflect the looks, the personality, or the demeanor of the parent? Regardless of how often we deny it, we each take pride in the traits and heritage that make up our family, and we long for them to continue. I believe God is no exception. He, as our Heavenly Father, desires for a spiritual heritage and anointing to be passed down from generation to generation.

Levites — The Next Generation

I believe God has established a "special order" for kids whose parents are called into full-time ministry. We find in scripture two orders of Jewish people in leadership, kings and priests.

God instructed the priests, also known as the Levites, to care for the temple and minister to the Lord on behalf of the entire nation of Israel. As they carried out their daily duties, making sure everything remained in order, their children followed and observed them. When their children reached a certain age, it became their responsibility to be the "pastors" over Israel. From this cycle in the Old Testament, I believe we can learn a few basic principles applicable to our lives in ministry today.

First and foremost, I believe God designed a spiritual heritage to be passed down. The ministers of Israel came specifically from the tribe of Levi, and from that lineage came each generation of priestly servants. The next generation of ministers came from within their own ranks.

Obviously it is not your children's responsibility to enter full-time ministry, for God may lead them in another direction. But regardless of what they may do, they will inherit an undeniable spiritual heritage. It's no wonder that Satan so desperately tries to influence the offspring of those who minister the gospel. Satan would love to put an end to the blessed heritage God has created in your lives.

P.K.'s typically take one of two approaches to the heritage they hold; they either view it as a blessing or a curse.

The Ministry-Heritage Blessing

I consider myself immensely blessed to be a part of a ministry family, and I'm not a rare exception. After surveying dozens of P.K.'s, we discovered that one of the top three things they like most about having parents in the ministry is that it has given them a deep spiritual heritage.[47]

98

No one intends for this spiritual heritage to be a curse, but as your P.K. grows in age, they may come to view it this way if you have not presented it to them from the perspective that a heritage is a true gift. By understanding that the enemy targets your children, you are then more aware of the need to work harder in keeping your own life close to the Lord.

Satan seeks to seduce your children away from their spiritual heritage.

Proverbs 6:26 states, "For by means of a whorish woman a man is brought to a piece of bread, and the adulteress will hunt for the precious life."[48] Satan plays the role of the adulteress in your life and within your family, and we're assured that he roams about seeking those whom he may devour. He wants to kill, steal, and destroy anything that brings glory to Christ. He seduced one third of the angels into leaving heaven, the safest most incredible place that exists. Rest assured that he wants to seduce your children out of their spiritual heritage for his own benefit.

The Hebrew translation of the word "precious" means valuable, beloved, and highly esteemed.[49] Satan translates that same word to mean: "danger to my kingdom," "future problem," and "specific target." Satan will do all that he can to target the "precious seed" the Lord has given you and try to turn them into cynical, rebellious individuals. It is our opportunity to protect, guard, and remind them of the incredible spiritual heritage that the Lord has given them.

Balancing Family and Ministry

When the balance of ministry and family gets skewed, then your children will most likely view the ministry that you consider to be a blessing as a curse. Pray with them, share your victories, do the little things that will keep your kids feeling like you, as a family, are in this together.

One well-known pastor wrote a declaration, which he then prayed over his children and grandchildren. He placed the declaration on the doors of their bedrooms as a visible reminder.

One evangelist's grandson takes the time to enter his grandpa's office every once in a while to read the testimonial letters to remind him of the lives being reached.

Yes, being in the ministry has some special challenges, but you never need to apologize to your children for the things that the Lord has called you to do. Instead, make it a priority to include your family. Let them always know that not only do they come first, but also they are a part of every victory, every testimony, and every new opportunity, because they are a part of you.

From simple moments to significant prayer times, let's look at a few of the tangible things you can do to create a sense of spiritual heritage in your children.

Establish a Family Creed

Fortune 500 companies, schools, churches, and ministries all establish mission statements, goals, and core values that every member of the organization learns and strives to uphold. Your family should be no exception. Granted, infants and toddlers may not fully understand upholding core values and working towards mission statements, but kids of all ages comprehend honesty, faithfulness, and hard work as important. My parents developed for us *The Mayo Family Creed*, and to this day it still reflects the core values that define who we are as a family and what we stand for or wish to be.

The night my parents presented our family creed to us, we were each given a framed shadow box with items that characterized who we are as individuals, old pictures, keys, my dad's high school ring, and other mementos. They still hang on our walls, reminding us of the cornerstone principles on which we build our lives. Each line my mom and dad read echoed the life that they'd already lived before us.

The Mayo Family Creed

Lovingly presented to Josh and Justin in August of 2000 as they transition into a new era in their lives. Given with the prayerful request that their eyes glance at these words often as a silent reminder of our family's most significant core values:

#1 – I alone ultimately control my own happiness by the attitudes I mentally fan in the private corridors of my mind. No circumstance or person can impact my personal happiness significantly. With the Lord's help, I am the master of my own attitude.

#2 – Daily time alone with the Lord, though sometimes unfeeling and routine, remain the cornerstone of my personal walk with Christ. This time is the "oxygen" of my spiritual life. Thus, I fight savagely for consistency here.

#3 – Small compromises, no matter how well rationalized, eventually lead to big consequences.

#4 – Show me your friends, and I WILL show you your future.

#5 – Without "whitewashing" sin, I choose to give grace to others (even when mental criticism would be valid and easy). I make this choice because I realize that Christ will ultimately judge me with the same level of love and mercy I give to others.

#6 – I recognize loneliness as God's cry for friendship with me.

#7 – Nothing I do in life half-heartedly is ever fun. Thus, fun in my life is not an activity but an attitude.

#8 – I remain painfully aware of my own shortcomings and weaknesses. Thus, I embrace correction and frequently utter the words, "I was wrong; I'm really sorry."

#9 – I honestly believe that I was not placed in this family by accident. I embrace the destiny and dreams for which my heritage has prepared me. I rejoice in being able to live with a purpose higher than myself. My purposes are eternal. Indeed, forever is a long, long time.

#10 – In a world of self-centeredness, I still choose to "throw the one starfish back in." In a world of pulpit religion, I pray to authentically be "Jesus with skin on" to those around me.

#11 – Though most of my friends will eventually come and go, I will remain deeply committed to my family. The Mayo Family stands as my God-given anchor and the "cheering squad" that is always in my corner.

#12 – Lastly, and in truth… HE IS NO FOOL WHO GIVES WHAT HE CANNOT KEEP TO GAIN WHAT HE CANNOT LOSE.[50]

We read through these together over dinner on August 10, 2000, and each of us signed the pieces of paper as a symbol of commitment. Since that date the creed and the commitment have remained the same, but an exciting addition has been made. On January 22, 2005 – my wedding day – my wife Monica also signed the creed.

What does your life stand for?

Think of the things that clearly reflect what your life stands for. It is not by accident that you have the spouse and the children whom God has given you. Your spiritual anointing and call into full-time ministry requires sincere and whole-hearted commitment to Jesus Christ. It may sound strange to take an entire evening to sign a piece of paper and boldly declare your stance. But rest assured, there is a target on your family, set there by Satan himself. Your children may not understand the darts of the enemy when they are young, but without question they will feel them.

Making Moments Memorable

Dear Pastor, as a P.K., if I could tell you one thing…

Make your kids feel important. Every Saturday night my parents would have my brothers and I do devotionals and skits, and then we'd play dominos as a family. They were some of the most memorable times of my childhood. - Vanessa Cobbs[51]

Every special day on the calendar became an excuse for my parents to make a memory. From Christmas to birthdays, they never hesitated to create a memory, and I look ahead to my life as a father someday, knowing I will do the exact same thing. My parents' desire and commitment to make many events in my brother's and my life a special occasion left a deep impression on us and prevented us from ever thinking that a significant day to us was just another day.

Birthdays

Birthday parties involved far more than just a cake, a few presents, and a card in the mail from grandma. When I reminisce on those celebrations, I think of the Mayo Olympics, city-wide scavenger hunts, a trampoline jumping contest in my living room, and no less than thirty-five or forty kids scattered all over the place. Needless to say, this required weeks of planning. I'm grateful for all my parents put up with on behalf of my brother and me, but the work and effort never showed on their faces as they excitedly poured their energies into making it our day.

I know it's hard to imagine a giant trampoline in your living room, but as I mentioned earlier it became a tradition at the Mayo house. To this day, we're infamous for carrying our furniture out to the front lawn and placing the trampoline in the living room right beneath the balcony. Teenagers climbed the stairs and lined up to jump. One by one they jumped while my mom repeatedly asked, "How do you spell lawsuit?"

I understand it takes work, money, and a lot of creativity, but together you and your children can create the same lifelong memories. Every year we began weeks before the big day arrived, and eventually we developed a system to our madness. Let me point out that what I honestly remember most is not just the specific activities or the amounts of presents, but the *time, the energy, and the concern* my parents put into the party. The method to our madness began with getting a class roster, picking a theme, and then strategically planning each aspect from the snacks to the games. In our teenage years, our parties simplified immensely, but the heart behind them did not. Mom and Dad wanted not just a big party or a big moment, but a significant one.

Christmas

The other time of the year that holds the most significance in our family is Christmas. For others it might be Easter or Thanksgiving. All families have their own special holidays, but in the Mayo household, every second of Christmas Day became a tradition. Each year we would have breakfast in bed. Then we would open certain presents first, while others were saved for last.

The principle in all of this is putting love and energy into the times that your children remember, thereby providing them with memories that make them proud to be yours. As a minister, the cares and concerns of the life you lead can drain you emotionally and physically. It's simple and even normal for birthdays, Christmas, and other holidays to get thrown together or swept under the rug.

Whatever you decide to do with your family, make sure they know your heart is in it and that your attention is completely focused on them. Times of late nights and stressful seasons inevitably creep up on any minister, but as you make these special times a priority, you make up for times when you were spread too thin.

Planning the Moment

Spontaneity can really add spice to life. Ideally every parent longs to seize a huge moment in their kids' lives the moment it happens. To insure you don't miss out, create the perfect moment through careful planning, and while the spontaneous ones still may occur, you'll never have regrets of what you wished you had done.

One Christmas, we did the typical breakfast in bed and then raced to the tree, only to see more presents than any two boys deserved. Near the end of the unwrapping chaos, my parents pulled out a special gift that apparently they'd been saving. As I opened the box, I noticed two silver dog tags mounted next to a picture of my grandfather, who had died when I was only two years old. He served at Pearl Harbor during World War II, and later took part in a famous mission off the coast of China during the Vietnam conflict. Inside the box lay a note from my mom about his heritage, character, and spirit becoming mine. No video game, no piece of clothing, not even a new car would have meant as much as that box of treasures did.

On another occasion, my parents presented me with my Grandfather Mayo's Dake Bible. He gave his life to the ministry, and my parents knew that it was also my dream to one day become a pastor. With each gift they were presenting to me a piece of their heritage, making it mine.

Marking the Milestones

Your children will take pride in who you are and what they're becoming, as you provide a few milestones along the way to solidify the process. When my parents gave me those dog tags and the Dake Bible, my heritage came to life.

Even if you don't have an antique or sentimental gift from your past, consider going to an antique shop and looking for something you could use to encourage or develop your child. The key to creating your own gift and moment is simply to make it meaningful!

Remember when you first started dating your husband or wife, and you presented them with different things you'd spent your time making or putting together, only to show them how much you cared? It might have been a journal you made for them, a collage of pictures, a box with little sayings, or a chest of special tokens. The principles haven't changed, so do that for your children.

For the rest of their life they'll be able to show their friends, their coworkers, and their future children, proudly telling how "this ring... this picture...this frame...this Bible..." was given to them by Mom and Dad. Beyond the actual gift, you've also given them a story to tell, and showed them it's the thought and heart that count.

THINK ABOUT IT...

1. Yes, being in the ministry has some special challenges, but you never need to apologize to your children for the things that the Lord has called you to do. Instead, make it a priority to include your family. What are some ways you could show your family that they are a part of every victory, every testimony, and every new opportunity, simply because they are a part of you?

2. We all long to pass on to our children the things we most deeply cherish. Ask yourself this question: *What do I most want our family to stand for?* Once you have answered that question, you are well on your way toward establishing your own family creed. You may also begin to think of gifts you could give your children

to symbolize what your family's spiritual heritage is all about. What gifts can you give as significant symbols of who you are?

3. What are some family traditions you wish to create? What do you want birthdays and holidays to look like in your family?

One of the many fun birthdays

Getting Grandpa Suddeth's dog tags for Christmas

**Monica adding her signature to the Mayo creed
on our wedding day**

CHAPTER 9

Dealing with the Dark Side
Of Ministry

By far the hardest thing that I had to deal with as a child in the ministry was living with the expectations that others had placed on my shoulders...not to mention the expectations I had placed on myself. - Anonymous P.K.

Some early American Indians practiced a unique ritual to train their young braves. On a boy's thirteenth birthday he learned to hunt, scout, and fish. When he'd successfully acquired each skill, he was put through one final test: to spend an entire night in the dense forest or bleak desert alone. This final challenge represented his first moments outside the security of his family and his tribe. A blindfold was placed over his eyes, and he was walked slowly into the wilderness where he was left alone in the darkness to overcome his fear.

When the boy finally senses the dawn break and sunlight entering his surroundings, it feels like an eternity has passed. And what the boy discovers when he takes off the blindfold is the familiar outline of someone standing a few feet away, armed with a bow and arrow. The boy felt alone in the dark, but the truth was, his father had been there all along.[52]

A life of service in the ministry can lead to many mountaintop experiences, but there is also a dark side of ministry. As P.K.'s, we need to know that our father and mother are in the wilderness with us, especially when it gets darkest and we don't feel there is anyone protecting us. In the midst of hard times, often you may be the only individuals who can lift the "unfair weights" of circumstances and events off of your children. Whether or not you ever release an arrow, we need to know that you, as our parent, are ready to respond in a moment's notice when we need your support. One of the most important areas where you can learn to protect your children is by teaching them how to deal with the "dark side" of expectations.

The Negative Expectation

Dear Pastor, as a P.K., if I could tell you one thing…

Kids become what others continuously label them…and if you do not negate the negative expectations others place on your child, you will get negative results. - Jonathan French[53]

If there is one thing most P.K.'s do not like, especially when they're teenagers, it is being labeled. We despise stereotypes, and many of our attitudes and actions directly reflect our great attempt to break them. While we want to fit into a specific social structure, the last thing we want is to be *told* where we fit.

We often hear the words "preps, jocks, nerds," and they all carry a specific connotation. Ministry kids carry a label all their own. You can try to deny it or blame it on someone's twisted or incorrect perception, but based on our survey of nearly one hundred P.K.'s, we found that the majority of them admitted they felt labeled and, in fact, they felt that the term "P.K." held a negative connotation.

P.K.'s were asked how they felt they were viewed:

23% - positively, 74% - negatively, 3% - neither[54]

Jarrod Cooper tells a humorous story that epitomizes what many would consider a typical P.K. stunt: "Communion had just been served in those ridiculously small cups Pentecostal churches use. Six hundred people waited while the pastor rattled off the same scripture he read at every communion service. He gave the nod and six hundred hands lifted six hundred little plastic cups of red communion juice to six hundred mouths. There was a rattling, a shuffling; then six hundred screaming Pentecostals ran for the toilets, throwing up on the walls and carpets, gathering around toilets, squeezing around wash basins. The sick were everywhere. Someone had added bleach to the juice mixture."[55]

It's precisely the kind of stunt that would be blamed on a P.K. often followed by words like rebellious, bitter, troublemaker, and wild. The frequent association and labeling of rebellious acts and attitudes to a typical P.K. is less than amusing. Put yourself in your son or daughter's position and try to imagine what it feels like to *always be expected* to be the bad kid.

Self-Fulfilling Prophecies?

Based on all the research, surveys, and interviews, we know it's not a myth; it's a fact. P.K.'s feel that they are viewed in a negative light, and this negative branding doesn't help you in your efforts to raise them to be strong men and women of God. Some P.K.'s earn their reputation, but the vast majority of them are unfairly labeled due to the behavior of a relatively small number.

What you say to your child, or allow others to say to your child, can eventually create a reality. Tell a P.K. they will have problems adjusting, and they'll have trouble adjusting. Tell them they will be just like the pastor's kid down the street, and you'll endure the same sleepless nights the pastor down the street is enduring. Be careful how much you allow your children to be compared to other P.K.'s who really do have serious problems.

111

Cameron Lee and Jack Balswick, two psychologists who have specialized in studying minister's families, would call this negative expectation a form of a "self-fulfilling prophecy."[56] People become what they are told, what they are expected to be. Once we're labeled as P.K.'s, it's quite difficult to remove those labels in our own minds as well as the minds of others. Self-fulfilling prophecies are dangerous to your children, and quite difficult to erase.

A funny thing happened on the way to the psych ward...

David Roshenhan[57] illustrates this principle in a study he conducted with a group of psychiatric patients: Eight mentally stable people, including three psychologists and one psychiatrist, were asked to pretend to have symptoms so they could gain admission into the psychiatric wards of several hospitals for treatment. During the initial interview, they falsified only three pieces of information: their name, their occupation, and the admission of hearing voices. All other questions about their personal background were answered truthfully. All were successfully admitted.

Once diagnosed and admitted, the eight people stopped faking all symptoms, but the staff never detected their deception. They continued to relate to the eight volunteers as bona fide psychiatric patients. Embarrassingly enough, many of the real patients could tell the difference. At times they voiced their suspicions strongly: "There's nothing wrong with you; you must be checking up on the hospital."

Rosenhan's point was clear. Once a diagnosis was made, even normal behavior was reinterpreted to match the clinical diagnosis. The people who evaluated the disturbed patients labeled them incorrectly. In the same way, prejudices regarding P.K.'s can result in them being treated as if they are going to rebel, whether or not it is a reality. These labels can come from other pastors, teachers, leaders, and parents. Usually those closest to a P.K. know the truth, but it's hard to convince the rest of the world.

Breaking Self-Perpetuating Cycles

Lee and Balswick explain, "To have expectations of a person's behavior is one thing. To have expectations based on a stereotype creates a self-perpetuating cycle: the stereotype feeds the expectations, and or expectations reinforce the stereotype."[58] While you may not be able to keep the stereotypes from being made, you as the parent can keep your child from believing them.

Would you ever allow anyone to tell your child that he is stupid, ugly, or even weird? Absolutely not! The biblical principle that life and death really are held in the power of the tongue is a reality. Don't allow yourself to be amused by it, or to accept it; take a stand against it. Recognize that this is something your children will deal with, and then begin to be proactive in protecting them from the negative expectations.

A children's evangelist, once said, "Many pastors' kids inherit a bad reputation before they even have the opportunity to demonstrate a specific behavior pattern, good or bad. It's assumed that P.K.'s are the worst kids in church." A few negative statements may not appear to be that devastating, but remember it's the "small foxes" that spoil the vine, as Scripture says. In reality, there are thousands of P.K.'s who have grown up in the ministry, honored their parents, and are now serving God full time.

Stereotype-Buster Arsenal

It is a good thing to be resolute and determined to challenge and equip your children to live for God. But keep in mind that a child's faith and a teenager's faith look and live differently than an adult's faith. Beware of using an adult measure to assess your child's faith level and spiritual maturity. Realistically keep in mind that your children *will not* be perfect, and be reassured they won't live a life directly opposite of what you've worked so hard to teach them.

How to protect your child from negative expectations? Continually remind them of how important they are to Jesus. Let them know when they look like Him, sound like Him, and do what He would do, that you are proud. They need your help to show them how God views them. This is what matters most. They'll learn not to concern themselves with what others think or say, when they realize who they are in Him and how much they mean to you.

Watch your levels of excitement in how you handle both the good and bad situations. Always reiterate to your children that you love them for who they are—not for what they do. Although you probably won't admit it, it is possible for us to focus a little too much on how your child's behavior reflects on the ministry leader. It's important to be sure to correct your kids out of the best interest of the child and not to enhance your own reputation or keep congregants happy. Sadly, many of us may have seen pastors sacrifice their children on the altar of people pleasing.

Don't Be an "Over-Expecter"
Dear Pastor, as a P.K., if I could tell you one thing…

Being a pastor's daughter is overwhelming at times…having parents who are understanding and patient is amazing.

- Heather Wheeler[59]

Some time ago, I came across a humorous cartoon that showed a fourth-grader apparently arguing with his teacher. Behind them, on the blackboard, were math problems the boy hadn't finished. The student looks directly at the teacher and says, "I'm not an under-achiever; you're an 'over-expecter'!"

Ask any kid whose parents are in some form of full-time ministry about expectations and be prepared to listen. We live in a society of over-expecters, but what makes the expectations placed on P.K.'s heavier than most is that the expectations come from people we love and see on a regular basis.

Without question, expectations aren't always a bad thing. In fact, at times they are necessary for setting the tenor and raising the bar on our attitudes and lifestyle. However, heed this warning: in the world of ministry, too many expectations placed upon your son or daughter can lead to a disastrous future.

Where do the expectations come from? I want to address the primary areas in which most ministry kids inevitably deal with over-expectation.

Family Over-Expectation

My parents believed in me as their kid, not as a P.K. We were just family. - Joy Delgatty[60]

Dear Pastor, as a P.K., if I could tell you one thing…
Give your kids realistic expectations. - Tom Barker[61]

All parents want their children to be the best they can be. There is nothing wrong with that. But in doing so you walk a fine line between what you envision to be their very best and the reality of what *actually is* their best.

Report card time is always traumatic for most children, even if they're good students. I still remember coming home late and walking in to see my dad and mom standing in the kitchen looking over the grades that had arrived in the mail earlier that day. They both would comment on how proud they were and how well I'd done, and then my dad would break into the infamous speech. "Josh," he'd say, "I made straight A's until the third grade." He always made a point to say, "I wasn't perfect in school, nor do I expect you to be."

We laughed about the "quarterly speech," but it always reassured me that his love for me was not based on what I did. It rested solely on who I was. With all the expectations your child will deal with outside your home, make sure you let them know you love them just for who they are.

Friendship Over-Expectation

Dear Pastor, as a P.K., if I could tell you one thing...

Please understand that, not only do we carry the weight of your expectations and the church's expectations, but even at times, the expectations of our friends. - Stephen Piersall[62]

One of the most difficult areas of expectations that a P.K. has to deal with is found within their friendships. Enduring expectations from peers only increases the weight of all the other expectations. Your son or daughter may not want his or her friends to feel like there is an extension of their pastor with them all the time, but the parents of their friends may not seem to mind.

A responsible P.K. can often be labeled as a second parent among peers. One P.K., whose father and grandfather are both in ministry, recalls feeling, in his teen years, as if he had to be a second set of parents for his friends. "When any of my friends were out with me, their parents never worried. They expected me to be just another parent," he admits. These expectations led him to a position of leadership among his peers that neither he nor they asked for.

Another college student, whose father had always been in full-time ministry, said, "Part of what I didn't like about Dad being in ministry was the expectations I dealt with in high school, the pressure to live up to them and perform a certain way."

This expectation usually begins when peers first find out that a guy or girl is a P.K. Established friends know to let go of this unfair measuring tool, but in the process of a P.K. making new friends, this stereotype can be difficult to overcome. New friends either don't know what to expect or they place the P.K. at a high standard, preventing them from feeling like they can relax and be themselves.

This leadership expectation may please you to some degree as a parent, because you desire for your son or daughter to be a leader, but it can make them resent it when it sets them apart from the rest of the group. Setting a standard and raising the bar are quite different from having the height of that bar already predetermined.

One girl remembers how much it bothered her growing up to hear, "Don't say that or don't do that around her, she's the preacher's kid." Another student admitted, "I hated being put up on a pedestal."

Most of us in ministry unanimously agree it's an incredible life, but we'd also agree that downsides still exist. As you think of the many ministry pressures that you have to deal with daily, please also plan to take the time to listen to your kids' concerns too. The psychological pressure they deal with is more than that of a normal child.

While other teenagers may worry about keeping their reputation clean, P.K.'s know that their life reflects not only them, but you and your entire ministry as well. They get tired of hearing about expectations, but walking the tightrope of living up to those expectations is far more exhausting. Be patient with your children, and love them, love them, love them.

Societal/Church Over-Expectation

When I was growing up in the church, people expected me to be a level above everybody else spiritually. - R.J. Tate[63]

Dear Pastor, as a P.K., if I could tell you one thing…
Don't let random people label your kids. Don't let the entire church become your kids' parents.
- Rachelle (Sumrall) Pagewood[64]

Dear Pastor, as a P.K., if I could tell you one thing…
Your kids really are who they are for God, not for you, your image, or the church. - Anonymous P.K.

Ninety percent of P.K.'s surveyed said they deal with unwanted expectations, and the place where they deal with it the most is within their own churches. A vast majority expressed that the expectations from their congregation and other church staff, greatly outweighed expectations at school, with peers, or with parents.

As a parent, relax and know that over-expectation by those in your church isn't your fault, nor is it something you can prevent 100%. One P.K. said, "I think our parents realize that we are just children too, but I don't think the congregation realizes this." Within the church world, most members respect, admire, and even want to get close to you as the minister. Your kids sometimes wind up being the gateway to understanding you as a person, or at least they are viewed that way.

Everyone is watching.

It seemed as I listened to the stories from countless P.K.'s that girls have a more difficult time than guys do. Their wardrobe choices are closely scrutinized, the amount of make-up they wear often comes into question, and their dating life always becomes everyone's business.

Part of living under a microscope means when your kids are late, everyone notices; when they talk during church, everyone hears about it. The examples are endless. How can you lessen the pressure placed on your children within the four walls of the church? The answer is simple: keep your family human.

It may seem like a small thing, but because you are a man or a woman whose words carry influence, use that influence to your advantage. Let the congregation know from the pulpit that your children aren't perfect, nor are theirs. It may not solve all your problems, but you'll take the weight off your kids and your congregation will feel better about their own family life.

Personal Over-Expectations

In truth, this is for some P.K.'s the biggest expectation battlefield - slugging it out with themselves. Depending on the personality of your son or daughter, the level of their personal expectations may vary, but I believe this is the hardest area for any of us to deal with. We are usually our own worst enemy and the mind games that race through our heads seem endless as we strive to do everything right.

Many times we P.K.'s are our own worst critic, especially when we have a strong spiritual heritage. We push and strive, always trying to be something more, knowing that as the children of those in ministry, we are supposed to care about people. Our parents' spirit of love and concern for souls often reproduces itself in us, and it becomes part of who we are. We want to care. We want to please. We want to be the best for everyone, including ourselves.

I remember growing up wanting desperately to do everything perfectly, to say the right things, act the right way, etc. I put pressure on myself, and when my own expectations weren't met, I felt like I had blown it. Most P.K.'s have very sensitive hearts toward the Lord. It's amazing the discernment we have in knowing when things aren't quite right in others, but this spiritual gift becomes detrimental when we realize we also don't measure up.

A certain older man, who is a thirteenth-generation Anglican priest, warns, "The psychological pressure is not to be underestimated. I was worried about failure." Falling short of perfection always precedes feelings of failure. What was considered a tender spirit, a spiritual gift, and strength, quickly disintegrates into weakness. The enemy wrestles with our thoughts and frustrations, verbalizing what we are already thinking: "You don't measure up. You really can't do this. You really are making your family look bad."

Do these mind games sound familiar? I'm sure these are all thoughts that have passed through your mind, and now Satan is using them on your children. You have much of the same fears and frustrations that your child has. With that thought in mind, realize that you are a big part of the solution:

- Talk to your children.
- Recognize that the greatest way to release the weight of expectations from your son or daughter is for you to personally lift that burden from them.
- Allow your children to see the part of you that has fought through these same areas of personal expectations.

Through your understanding and love, your children will be able to transfer that same understanding of grace and love to their heavenly Father.

I can't emphasize it enough that expectations in and of themselves are quite necessary. As a parent, you need to find the proper balance of expectations and reality. The idea is not to eliminate expectations, but to manage expectations fairly.

Capitalize on the fact that you can empathize with your children through understanding the unrealistic expectations that a congregation often places on them. Doesn't the pressure of running a successful ministry, counseling countless adults, establishing the church's financial security, and dissecting the entire Word of God in a three-week series, all while being a great spouse and parent, ever get to you sometimes? When the unrealistic expectations come, make sure the ministry remains a place where your child is not stifled, but instead is a place where they can grow and flourish.

THINK ABOUT IT...

1. *"People become what they are told, what they are expected to be."* Self-fulfilling prophecies are dangerous for children and are quite difficult to erase. Do you see any labels or over-expectations directly affecting your kids negatively? How will you counteract this?

2. *"I think our parents realize that we are just children too, but I don't think the congregation realizes this."* Within the church world, most members respect, admire, and even want to get close to you as the minister. Your kids sometimes wind up being the gateway to understanding you as a person, or at least they are viewed that way. What are some "expectation busters" you will use to help your congregation view your children accurately and your children view the congregation accurately?

3. One of the greatest ways to release the weight of expectations from your son or daughter is to personally show them how you allow Christ's grace to help you in all you do. How well are you modeling a reliance on Christ's grace?

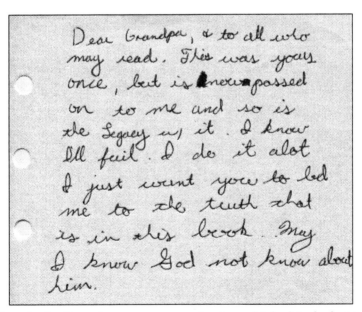

A note to Grandpa – a moment where I tried to balance the weight of expectations…

CHAPTER 10

Warning: Pitfalls Ahead

When I hear the word "pitfall" I think of one wonderful thing – the invention of the Atari 2600 Game System. To my knowledge, the Atari 2600 was basically the first gaming system that was sold worldwide to play on your TV. Ok, I'll admit it; I personally would not know what to do if the Lord did not allow this beautiful game system to grace my hands when I was young boy. It gave me hours of entertainment, and even as I write this I wonder what it would cost for me to own the Atari 2600 again.

Of all the games that you could play on the classic Atari system, my all-time favorite was called *Pitfall!* Let me explain how the game was played, for those of you who missed this glorious opportunity. The main character was Pitfall Harry. You were to help him avoid dangerous pitfalls, deep lakes, alligators, scorpions, open camp-fires, and rolling logs in an unforgiving jungle. The goal was to collect as many gold and silver bars and diamond rings as possible in the brief time allotted.

If you were to read the actual instruction manual for that game today (which I have, of course…thank you very much!), it gives you a warning to not "…start such a difficult journey without reading this manual first very carefully." If you were to avoid the common pitfalls in the game, you would have to know what they looked like and how to get past them.

There are also pitfalls unique to P.K.'s. Ok...I'll admit it...these pitfalls are very different than an old Atari game, but the application is obvious. If these pitfalls for P.K.'s are addressed, we are less likely to see our kids fall prey to them. Sadly, when these pitfalls don't get addressed, the opposite will be true. Here are four practical ways you can help your children live a more stable life, guarding them against the pitfalls that lie ahead:

#1 – Let your child's talents be theirs, not yours.
Dear Pastor, as a P.K., if I could tell you one thing...

Know that your child's calling in life might not be the same as yours - Ashleigh Hancock[65]

Dear Pastor, as a P.K., if I could tell you one thing...

Support your kids' dreams, whether they be ministry or a job in the secular workforce. God has created each as an individual, so support your child in that - Jason Mc Cutchen[66]

One of the keys to raising children in the ministry is consistently encouraging and nurturing the talents the Lord places in their lives. My parents never actively sought to have their talents and abilities be replicated in my life, nor did they expect me to be good at the same things that came naturally to them. For example, you may be a fantastic communicator, but your son or daughter may not be. Or, simply, because you're anointed in the area of worship doesn't mean you should pressure your children to be involved in music. Unspoken pressure to become just like their father or mother should not shout loudly in the minds of P.K.'s.

Encourage the different gifts you see in your children, especially the gifts that are different from your own. To this day, I can remember the times when my mom encouraged me specifically in areas that she recognized as "Josh" strengths. She would comment on things like my computer graphic abilities or certain creative flairs that I had that she didn't feel particularly strong in. She would often compliment me and would go as far as to say that I would surpass her in those areas. I'm grateful for her words and hope to live them out.

#2 – Let your kid be a kid.
"I had to be an adult long before I ever was."

- Anonymous P.K.

This does not mean giving your children a license to do whatever they want, nor does it mean you should not discipline them. We all understand that freedom without responsibility breeds rebellion. But many parents expect their child to behave like an adult, especially when "everyone's watching." Your kids already know that they carry the weight of reflecting the person behind the pulpit. You don't have to remind them. Create a balance in your family that exemplifies discipline, but allows them to act thirteen when they are thirteen. To give a small example, my parents learned early on that it's pretty hard to keep three- and five-year-old boys still and quiet on the front row for an evening service. We had already gone through our fill of church for the day, and let's just say that we would get a little "squirmy." Instead of "Pastor Mom and Pastor Dad" making the three- and five-year-olds act like eight- and ten-year-olds, my parents did the right thing. Mom sat with us a few rows back from the front where we colored and played with games to our hearts' content. We were no longer a distraction to others, and we were no longer bored out of our minds. It seems like a simple idea, but honestly, many pastoral parents would think twice before allowing it because of the possible perception from others of, "Look, the pastor's kids are acting like…like…kids."

Sharon Collins says, "In their desire to help their kids maintain high moral standards, ministers may also shelter their children too much. Ministers are exposed to so many hardships caused by sin and mistakes. We don't want our kids to be exposed to them.

But being overprotective may actually push them toward greater rebellion and make them more vulnerable by keeping them more naïve."[67]

No child automatically knows the exact thing to do in every situation, and there will be times when they make a wrong decision. It's never wrong to expect your kids to be good kids, but always keep in mind that they are still just kids.

#3 – We aren't free labor.

Dear Pastor, as a P.K., if I could tell you one thing…

Forcing your children to be actively involved could be a problem. Fortunately my parents never pushed ministry involvement on us, so we enjoyed being involved - Heather Wheeler[68]

When we first started the church, we all came in on Saturdays and were the temporary janitors for a while. None of us enjoyed it, but when something needed to be done at church, we were the only ones who weren't allowed to say no. - Caleb Piersal[69]I

This is incredibly important, and quite frankly it's an area where many ministers innocently fall short. Richard Willowby, the writer of *Prodigal P.K.s, "What Happens When the Children of Ministers Go Wrong?"* warns against this trap. "Some ministers only increase this pressure," he says. "If teenage P.K.'s feel they must sing in every youth group concert or live flawlessly because they exist in the spotlight of their parents' vocation, they may want to escape the glare of expectations. That desire may grow even stronger if the family's commitment to church life rules out other interests such as athletics or drama."[70]

Get a group of P.K.'s together and ask them what it feels like to be the permanent back-up for everything. "Free labor," echoes through their real-life accounts. In many churches, the pastors' children are often found doing janitorial work, helping with youth, working in the nursery, greeting congregants, mowing the lawn, and even on stage leading worship when worship team members don't show up.

While nudging your children into full-time ministry, doing that by forcing their service usually ends in disaster. My parents always allowed it to be our decision. We never hesitated to become involved at the church, but it felt good knowing it was always our choice. We perceived every capacity in which we served as an opportunity to support our church and its vision, not as a dreaded duty we did because we were P.K.'s and we "had to."

#4 – Address the expectations of others.
Dear Pastor, as a P.K., if I could tell you one thing …

Teach your children to have a relationship with Christ, not religious standards to live by because they have to be examples. - Aaron Hellfinstine[71]

Dear Pastor, as a P.K., if I could tell you one thing…

Being forced to be involved or even to be the perfect little Christian is what has pushed me away at times. Balance is the key.
- Anonymous P.K.

Did you know that you're not the only parents your kids will have? Whether you like it or not, your congregation or those involved in your ministry feel it is their collective duty to raise your son or daughter. Trust me, this is not an opinion it is a fact to admit, to accept, and to address. I, along with so many others, felt I had to walk, talk, and act in a certain "preacher's son" way, mainly because of how members of the congregation would sometimes try to "help" parent me, even though their intentions were always good. Parents, please notice when others are trying to play a role in our lives that isn't needed, and do something about it.

Is it about my kids... or me?

Think of all the expectations others have for your children, including the unrealistic ones. Consider the pressure you feel to have your children tow the line of those expectations. Examine your motivation. Do you want them to live up to the expectations in their best interests, or are you concerned with how their performance affects your reputation?

Sometimes what is best for your children may not be fun or even what you feel like doing. In spite of all this, keep in mind that trying to please everyone is the first step to failure. You are first a parent and secondly a minister.

A survey in *Leadership* magazine found that 94% of pastors feel pressured to have an "ideal family."[72] That's a lot of pressure. No matter how hard you try, your congregation will always view you differently. Still, there are things you can do to help your kids bear up under the pressure and function in their high-expectation environment.

In all of this, communication remains crucial. Talk to your kids about the expectations others are placing on them. Let them know that you are aware of the unrealistic expectations of others and the pressure they must feel sometimes. Let them know you love them and that you don't hold them to these same expectations.

Make sure you communicate that the intentions and heart of others are sincere. Be sure to tell your children you love them and that you are ready to listen and help them deal with the frustrations they'll encounter. If you can't free them from the trial, you can at least help them navigate through it.

THINK ABOUT IT...

1. One of the keys to raising children in the ministry is to consistently encourage and nurture the talents the Lord places in their lives. What talents and abilities need to be nurtured in your child?

Are you helping to nurture these, or are you encouraging your child to fill a need of the church instead?

2. Create a balance in your family between discipline and just letting kids be kids. If you don't accurately understand common cognitive or developmental capabilities children their age should exemplify, look for a course on developmental psychology, or find a Christian author who has studied those topics to help you accurately assess what are typical behaviors for children at each age level. But simply put, how well are you doing at letting your kids be kids?

3. What pitfalls do you believe your children are most likely to fall into? What is one thing you will do this week to help your kids avoid one of those pitfalls?

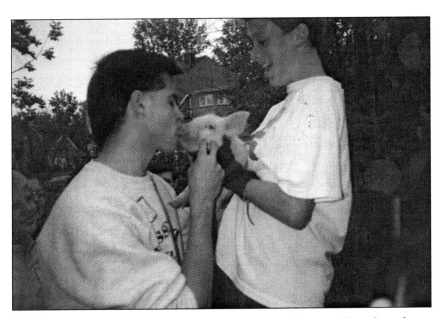

Letting me be a kid even if it meant holding a kiss the pig competition at my birthday party…with that clearly defined on each invitation sent out

**Traveling with a drama team for the summer…
the ministry of my choice as a kid**

Soccer, our favorite sport

CHAPTER 11

Life After the Train Wreck

It hit hard, harder than I expected. Well, I guess that was part of the problem. I didn't expect it at all. My family now fondly refers to this time period as "The Train Wreck." We all know that life in general and ministry in particular always comes complete with its "tough times." But this chapter focuses on helping your children overcome times that are far more challenging than the normal tough times along the way. That's why I refer to them as "train wreck moments."

For us, our "train wreck moment" came late in the game. My brother and I were nearly raised, and though there had been obvious rough spots along the journey, the Lord had graciously spared us from any devastatingly big ones. Then about midway though my brother's university training and near the conclusion of my preparation for my future, the train wreck occurred.

My parents had pastored a wonderful church for over thirteen years. My mom had run both the youth ministry and the church's private school. My dad served as its senior pastor. To make a very long story short, they began to hear that "board members wanted them out." The bottom line was that some key board members felt the adult church congregation was not growing quickly enough.

Our church was not a small one by any standard. It had a wonderful congregation of over 2,000 people who attended each week. My brother and I had done all our growing up there. Mom would often smilingly say, "This is the home our family has had most of our memories in, and this will be the home we'll still be living in one day when we retire." For thirteen incredible years, we had pastored this exceptional church and "done life together." Because we were miles away from our extended family, the church had become our family. Our friends were there. Our memories were there. The majority of our spiritual growth had happened there. In short, the roots went very deep.

The End of a Ministry

I don't suppose I can adequately communicate the pain that occurred when my mom took me aside to gently say, "Dad and I are going to submit our resignation." I went numb. This really couldn't be happening. I just knew it was a bad dream and that soon I would wake up to find it had all gone away. But days later, I realized that "the train wreck" had come in all of its deafening force and had come to stay. Both of my parents had been in full-time ministry at the church, and suddenly all that was gone.

My heart pivoted from anguish to fury. "This is so unfair, Lord," I remember saying. For as long as I could remember, I had sensed the call of God on my life, quietly directing me. But amidst "the train wreck," I told my parents that I was no longer sure about my future goals. I can remember standing in our kitchen, choking back tears and telling my mom, "I don't think I have tough enough skin to be able to survive a life of ministry if this is what can happen to you." My brother had similar feelings.

It was Christmas time when we discovered the extent of my brother's pain. Our parents had worked hard to make the holidays seem "normal." But finally, at our family Christmas dinner, my college-aged brother blurted out, "Look, none of you will ever know how close I've come to walking away from all of this and I do mean all of this. I just couldn't do it because I knew it would cause even more pain for the family." He broke into tears at the Christmas dinner table as the rumblings of the continuing "train wreck" left an indelible impression on our lives that year.

Let Love Lead

I can remember marveling at how my parents responded to this situation so meekly and silently. My brother and I just felt that they had let certain people off the hook way too easily. They were determined to avoid splintering the church, so they chose to resign "in mutual agreement with the church board and for reasons of desiring further numerical growth." Boy, did I have that line memorized. And it was a truthful line.

Our particular church government structure called for the church board to bring the matter to a vote of the entire church. The people dearly loved my parents, so it seemed very clear to all of us what the results of the vote would be. But my parents would not allow it. They refused to put the church they loved through the pain and drama. They felt impressed by the Lord to follow the wisdom of Solomon.

Remember when the two mothers came to Solomon, both claiming that the baby was theirs? Solomon ordered for the baby to be cut in half, and one woman immediately objected. She was willing to give up her rights to the child in order for it to be unharmed and remain alive. Then Solomon's response to the situation was to give that woman the baby. Why? Because he knew that the true parent would never allow the child to be harmed.

During the early train wreck days when my brother and I repeatedly called for "justice" and to "let the people decide," my parents would hear nothing of it. They loved the church dearly and wanted to make sure nothing splintered or hurt its congregation. I remember on several occasions overhearing my parents tell people to stop petitions and all other forms of complaint.

On the morning they resigned, they even used the church's deep love for them to further make the transition as easy as possible. I remember my father's broken words to the church, "If you really love Jeanne and myself, the way you can best prove your love is by staying here and supporting the board and new leadership that comes." I can remember everything inside of my head yelling, *Stop making this whole thing easier on the people who have caused this pain!*

In my pain, I remember secretly feeling good at the prospect of things going a little rough after we left, almost as a means to validate our worth. But my parents, though honest with the depth of their hurt, continued to remind us that, "It is not so much what happens TO us; but more importantly, what happens IN us." They never whitewashed the situation, because Justin and I were much too old to be fooled into thinking that it was "no big deal." But on the other hand, they were determined to respond in love instead of out of retaliation.

Harm done at the hands of God's people: It does happen.

I'm sure no one in the ministry ever really expects to get broadsided by the one area that you have given your life to, the ministry and God's people. But it happens. Sadly, it happens more than I or any other ministry leader would care to admit.

It hurts when you give your life so unselfishly to an area that you feel the Lord has called you to and in one brief moment, "the train wreck" happens. In a single moment, your whole world changes. The person, institution, group, or ministry that you have so unselfishly given yourself to for possibly numerous years unexpectedly seems to "roll over you." You try to console yourself with the fact that the resulting changes might be God's bigger plan for you. I don't doubt that such might well be the truth in some of these situations. But despite all this, it still does not compensate for the devastating manner in which the painful situation can unfold.

Facing the Train Wreck as a Family

During this season, our home was left with aching that went beyond description and pain, which did not easily disappear. If such a train wreck happens in your ministry, you may find that, all too quickly, the friends that you have given your life to seem to evaporate. And one morning, in the midst of "the train wreck," you wake up with an agonizing sense of aloneness, anger, and despair. How can you best survive? The family must pull together.

Whether you are in the church as a full time minister or a volunteer with a full-time heart, there are numerous things that could be listed as train wreck moments. A church dispute, change in pastoral leadership, a sudden divorce, betrayal by staff or friends, serious health difficulties, job termination, false accusations, a moral failure; the list could go on and on. Even the Son of God had "train wrecks" in His ministry and promised us the same.

Do any of these scenarios sound familiar to you? I hope not, but the sad truth is that if you stay in ministry long enough, there is high probability that a major "train wreck" of some sort will impact your family in the ministry.

Living and Loving Through the Train Wreck

What do you do during those unforgettable appointments with pain? As I write these next few pages, I pray that you will never find it necessary to reread them in the wake of your own personal family train wreck. But please read these thoughts carefully, my friend. Because how you as a parent handle the "train wreck moments" will have everything to do with whether your children survive them in one piece or as shattered, bitter people. Even as I write this chapter, a flood of buried emotions comes crashing back in. But with the help of a loving heavenly Father and unselfish, praying parents, both my brother and myself have "made it to the other side" to become stronger Christians than we ever were before.

Here are a few vital things my parents did, amidst their own deep hurt, to get through the train wreck, and to help my brother and me come out of this experience on top.

#1-Get inside the head of your P.K.

When the "train wreck" hits, gently make consistent efforts to find out what is going on inside your P.K.'s heart and mind. Don't push or pry, but just make it very easy for him or her to talk.

Creating a safe atmosphere for your children to openly talk about what they are feeling is one of the first steps for reconstructing after the brokenness. The moment you ask, "What's really going on in your head?" and "What are you really feeling?" you give them the freedom they need to let it all loose, expressing how they really feel.

There have been times when I have expressed my hidden feelings to my parents about one of our family's train wreck moments. They have heard statements from my brother and me like, "If this is how the ministry treats those who give everything to it, I don't want it!"

All my life I have personally wanted to impact and touch people's lives. During some of these painful moments I found myself questioning if that was something that I still wanted to "take a chance" on. I felt that I simply couldn't and wouldn't allow myself and my family to get hurt like my parents and family had just been hurt.

A couple of weeks after everything had "hit," I remember when my brother called me into my parent's bedroom, pulled me into his arms and started to cry uncontrollably. The train wreck was just beginning to take its toll on the Mayo boys.

Through these dramatic moments as well as through the months ahead, my parents continued to make it easy for us to talk. They didn't try to give sermons or easy answers. They weren't overly reactive or pushy. They just allowed us to vent without making us feel like we were wrong for doing so. They made sure that any time we wanted to talk, they were always available. Beyond that, they tenderly asked at key moments, "What's going on in your head?" They never pushed us or forced us to open up. They consistently made sure that we didn't have to bottle our emotions up on the inside, not even in the name of being "like Jesus."

We were given clear directions that we could not talk about these feelings "outside the family," because my parents wanted to bring no division in the church.

Build the bridge of communication now.

You may be wondering why Justin and I were so willing to open up to our parents to share what was actually going on inside. The answer is simple: My parents had practiced sensitive, nonjudgmental listening for years. They never pried or pushed, but instead, as they were raising us, they made sure they always took time to find out what was going on deep inside of us.

Unfortunately, many parents hesitate to "really talk and listen" until the big train wreck moments come. When this occurs, your child will be far more hesitant to open up and talk. Build bridges of communication during the normal times of life. Even if it is about something seemingly insignificant, it may be important to them. Topics like a hobby, problems at school, or a romance dilemma may seem trivial to you, but if you don't talk to them now, it is very likely that they won't feel free to open up to you in more difficult times.

Dear Pastor, as a P.K., if I could tell you one thing...

I cannot stress the importance of communication between you and your children, especially during the hard times. If you can keep them talking to you, you will ultimately win most any battle.

- Seth Macintosh[73]

#2-Empathizing With Your Kids' Pain: Saying "I'm sorry."

When the "train wreck" hits, tell your child how sincerely sorry you are that they are having to go through this experience.

Just saying a sincere "I'm so sorry" is a big step in minimizing the long-term damage of the train wreck. Letting your son or daughter know that you think it "stinks" too really does make a difference. Many times we kids just want to know that you think what's going on is wrong, too. Although our attitudes may be out of perspective, we just need you to be sorry for the times of turmoil, anger, and sadness that we are genuinely feeling.

When you say, "I'm sorry," you are not necessarily taking responsibility for the situation. You probably had little or nothing to do with it. But as a caring parent, you are acknowledging the depth of the pain and saying that you are so sorry that your child is experiencing it as well.

Remember that, at the cross, Jesus "took the rap" for the sins of the universe. He never deserved to have to make the unselfish moves that He did. He did it as an expression of the Father heart of God. In like manner, good earthly parents often say, "I'm sorry" to their children even when, from a human perspective, such is certainly not necessary.

As a teenager, I remember having my heart broken and feeling like I'd disappointed so many people in our church. I'll never forget finally telling my dad everything. He simply held me and just said, "I'm sorry it hurts." – Lesley (Piersall) Butcher[74]

#3- Make sure your kids hear you say words like, "I hurt too."

Only you as a family will truly understand the specifics regarding your own personal hard time. While each family member's reaction may be different, remember that everyone experiences the situation in his or her own way. Don't ever allow your child to feel alone in their hurt.

It is healing to know that your parent is being honest about their feelings during the train wreck times. The degree of that honesty is obviously tied to the specific situation and the age of the children.

But at bare minimum, let your child know simply that you hurt too. Sometimes in a parent's well-intentioned attempts to shelter their children, they totally deny the pain of a situation. This leaves the P.K. feeling shut out and leaves the parents looking very phony.

Though it is good to share, it is important to avoid saying too much and forcing your child to carry you emotionally. Children should not become their parents' "shrink" or counselor at these moments. That is far too much weight for them to bear. Nor should the child become the "venting place" for a parent's own raw emotions or pain. Such is very negative as well. A child should not be burdened with the details of what has happened. There should be more talked about in your home than the train wreck. Strike a wise balance.

It is healthy for your child to get some glimpses of your pain to see how you are dealing with it. Tell your child that you are hurting too, but also let them know and see how you are choosing to heal. Common ground builds bonds of closeness, understanding, and healing. That common ground will probably not be found with anyone else at school or church. Far beyond the sympathy others may try to offer, it will be your understanding that your children will need most.

One word of caution: If your personal train wreck involves unfaithfulness on the part of the other parent, be very sensitive as to how much you communicate with your child about the specifics. Never make them feel like you are asking them to "choose sides." No matter how great the sin of the other parent, it is important that you handle this type of situation with deep sensitivity, unselfishness, and maturity.

Take time to heal.

In all train wreck situations, the parents themselves will need to seek their own healing. Though you need to express your hurt honestly to your P.K., it is important that you not use them as your primary talking point. I remember my mom driving hundreds of miles so she could meet with a friend to "spill everything." Dad and she would take long walks out of the house where our ears could not hear them as they talked and cried together. Late at night, Mom would journal her thoughts to the Lord, needing a place to be able to empty herself on a daily basis without fear of being misunderstood.

Whatever the situation, admit honestly your own pain. But never do it in any manner that would further energize negative pain on your child's behalf.

#4-Guard the reputation of God.

Unlike Job's wife, who in a moment of weakness advised Job to "curse God and die", when the train wreck hits, pay close attention to what your words and actions are telling your kids about God's character and goodness. His faithfulness is amazing, especially during hard times. He is our constant refuge and our strength. But when we become a part of a train wreck that somehow deals with the church or our ministerial parents, it's only too easy for us to pin some of the blame on God.

Though your children may not verbalize these thoughts to you, they will probably be thinking, "How could a loving God ever let this happen to us?" or, "How can this whole Christianity thing be real if this occurred?" or, "If Jesus were real, He would have answered my prayers and made this whole thing come out differently." Even if you feel that your son or daughter is securely grounded in their relationship with Christ, they will quite possibly still hold God somewhat responsible for their pain, even if on a subconscious level.

God works all things together for our good ... eventually.

We all know that God "causes all things to work together for the good of those who love God," (Romans 8:28)[75] but that doesn't mean that all things start out good. So, please avoid the temptation of trying to explain everything down to a simple faith formula. Sometimes the most powerful thing you can say is, "I don't understand why all of this has happened. I don't even know how it is all going to work out. I just do know that faith still works. So during this time that we need Jesus more than we've needed Him in a long time, let's not let the questions push us away from Him. He loves us, and someday (maybe not until eternity), we'll get all the puzzle pieces from His perspective."

I remember late one December evening, at the height of our train wreck, finding my mom downstairs, still awake, reading her Bible. I plopped down on the couch next to her and blurted out, "How are we going to come through this?" Earlier that day, a future job opportunity had evaporated on us due to another "knife" being thrown in our direction. When I asked this question, Mom looked up, put the Bible down, and smilingly said, "I'm not sure of much of anything right now, Josh. But the one thing I am sure of is that God is still on our team, and faith in Him still works."

Often through the years, my parents have defined true faith as "Trusting in the character of God even when you do not understand His actions." Ever heard the old Christian song that says, "When you can't trace His hand, trust His heart?"[76] Well, during crisis seasons like these, realize that your P.K.'s will be looking hard to see how much you truly "trust His heart." They will need to see your faith remain steadfast no matter how great the shaking. So, talk over your own faith struggles with another trusting adult, but make sure you take care of how our heavenly Father may appear in the eyes of your P.K. If you don't care about those perceptions, I guarantee that Satan will do his best to use this situation for his long-term advantage.

#5-Help your child avoid over-generalizing.

During the train wreck, your child may want to write off "the church" and everything that surrounds it. Gently challenge them not to allow one very painful situation to transfer unfairly to all other similar institutions and/or people in their lives.

One of the main reasons P.K.'s rebel is because they are hurt or disappointed by people in the church. Growing up, I think I knew too much about church politics and the junk that surrounded it. To this day, it still makes it tough to be open in certain situations and to certain ministries. - Anonymous P.K.

Showing me that rough times within our church were not a reflection of God or His church was one of the biggest steps my parents took to help me personally come out of our challenging time unharmed. Everywhere I look these days, people seem particularly cynical against church, church leaders, and church politics. My parents often reminded us that, "There are politics anywhere there are people." I came to understand that politics and unfair treatment are prevalent anywhere that people work or congregate together, simply because we are all sinners who need the grace of God to rise above such behavior.

Dear Pastor, as a P.K., if I could tell you one thing ...
Make sure your child realizes the difference between religion and relationship, and that people will always let you down, but God's love is unfailing! - Anonymous, P.K.

We've all heard statements such as, "If this is what the church is like, then I don't want any part of it." My parents would address immediately anything that even remotely sounded like such an attitude. They would quickly respond with, "No, it's not the church (or a certain denomination). It's just people." They would go on to say that church people are mere humans like all of us. They mean well, but they are still people who can cause great pain at times. My parents also reminded us that we should never judge the many by the few. By protecting us against negative perceptions about Christ or His church, my parents minimized the long-term damage of our train wreck.

#6-At all costs, never allow resentment and bitterness to take up residence in your heart.

My dad never spoke bad about anyone—not people, ministries or other pastors. - Ruth (Daugherty) Sanders, P.K.[77]

In a good way, I have gotten sick of the many times that my parents have told me that "Everyone means well, and no one is being bad." One night at supper I laughingly responded, "If no one's being bad, then why is everything so messed up?" My parents have done their best not to allow me the "luxury" of becoming bitter toward anyone. I have quickly learned that when you allow someone who isn't acting very "Christian" to stand between you and God, that person is actually standing in a position closer to God than you are.

My mom defines resentment as, "Allowing someone who has hurt you to live rent-free in your mind." How do you get your kids to release the bitterness that they may feel? The hard truth is that we as children often reflect what we sense that you as our parents are feeling. So, if you want us to live free from the chains of unforgiveness and resentment, then you as our parents need to honestly face those issues yourself. Most of the time we just reflect what we sense or are seeing modeled by our parents. If you want us to let go of our resentment, you are going to have to take the lead first. Always remember that your children will be ok if they believe that you are ok.

#7-Remember, the Lord always honors those who choose to take the "high road."

Many ministers speak of raising the bar to a higher standard in our jobs, our families, our devotions, etc. But sadly enough, sometimes those same ministers don't hold themselves to that standard when problems arise and the pressure is on. Through the years, I have lost track of the number of times one of my parents, during a difficult moment, has commented, "We're taking the 'high road' on this one." As a matter of fact, I think they've pretty much always been "high road people."

Your children will be impressed by your high standards in ministry. But even more, they will be most impacted by your high standards of character. Reflecting on some of God's greatest champions in this era, you will often find they are the last to speak ill of anyone, often encouraging and blessing even those who have hurt them.

One thing I appreciate most about my dad is that I've never heard him say a negative thing against or about anyone.

– Nathan Piersall[78]

Anytime anyone approached us in public or were brought up in private, my dad always said, 'What a privilege and honor it is to love people.' We say we love people as a family and we really do.

- Anonymous P.K.

The toughest tests of your integrity will come when the difficult times of ministry hit you. Remember that not only must you come out of the fire stronger, but also it is precisely during those times when your children desperately need you to be an example of excellence. You have to take the high road. And this high road must be the one most often traveled by you, not the road less traveled.

This road gives honest compliments to people who have hurt you. It speaks well of those who have caused you pain, even when the door is closed and you could easily say something very different. It refuses to "spear" your personal King Saul even if you find him one night defenseless and asleep in a cave. In short, taking the high road in the midst of your family's train wreck means a costly choice to "live louder than you preach."

Dear Pastor, as a P.K., if I could tell you one thing ...

Never slander other ministers or any other leaders. Don't even discuss them in a negative light, and always remain positive towards the situation. - Sarah (Daugherty)Wehrli[79]

#8-Help your child see "obvious" signs of God's continued faithfulness.

Are you ready for another Mayo family quote? Our family is full of them, but this one would rank very high on our family's Top Ten list. It simply says, "God will be no man's debtor." Try reading it again. It's worth it. Put simply, God will never allow your biblical responses to go unrewarded.

Yet, once we have come through to the other side of the train wreck, it is easy to lose focus on the many ways that God's faithfulness has carried us through the situation. So please, pastor, look for any way you can to sincerely brag on the Lord as you choose to take the high road. Brag on how God's road really is the best road. Remind your family that because you attempted to respond to the rough times in a biblical fashion, God has lovingly taken care of you. Make sure they know that faith really does work.

Your child needs to know that God truly rewards people who handle their character correctly. Others may have tried to shade your character or make your life difficult for no reason, but you didn't take "low blows" at the offenders. They may have hurt your family very deeply. Your character may have been temporarily shaded by untrue rumors that were spread, but you took the high road and now God will reward you.

God is faithful ... always.

God truly is faithful. When your family has gone through the storm and begins to smile again, it's crucial that you point out the Lord's faithfulness through the ordeal and any possible positive fruits that came out of the situation. The Old Testament is full of examples in which the Israelites trusted God to protect, provide, and carry them through situations. Each time He proved Himself faithful, they built an altar, something tangible, so that later generations could be visibly reminded of why they serve the One True God. After God has brought your family through a difficult time, find something tangible and hold it up before your children. This is not to remind them of the pain, but to remind them of His promise. He is forever faithful!

A year after our train wreck Christmas, our parents announced that we were all going to buy small but symbolic gifts for each other, gifts that reminded us what we had learned during the previous difficult season. After we shared our symbolic gifts, we all took communion together around the Christmas tree. It was a very different Christmas than the one we had celebrated the year before. But both Justin and I will never forget the very clear picture we received of the fact that, "All things really do work together for good for those who love the Lord," even for those of us who wear invisible t-shirts that read, "I Survived the Train Wreck."

Dear Pastor, as a P.K., if I could tell you one thing...

Always know and always remind your children of this one truth: that God will be no man's debtor. - Justin Mayo, P.K.[80]

THINK ABOUT IT...

1. No one expects a "train wreck." But, that may be the reason why so many Christians fall completely to pieces when they hit. Write down some ways you would ideally like to help your family cope, and how you personally would like to handle any potential train-wreck scenarios. (You're not planning for the negative here but writing about WHO you'd like to be during those painful moments both personally and as a family when or if they hit.)

2. Are you really building bridges of communication with your children *now*? Don't wait until the train wreck moments to ask your children how they are really doing. What can you do today to build a stronger bridge?

3. Reflecting on the points made in this chapter, and using the peace of today to help prepare for potential "train-wreck" moments that may come tomorrow, ask yourself, "Which of these areas could I personally strengthen right now?"

Having fun as a family – even after a train wreck

A really good day...life really does go on

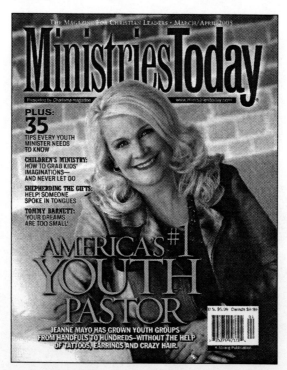

**Another reason I'm so proud of my Mom...
a secret reminder to us that God really is faithful
even after a train wreck**

CHAPTER 12

What Should I Do If My Kid Goes South Spiritually?

Why does it so often seem that those who live closest to the ministry are sometimes the ones who struggle most to feel close to God? Raising kids in the ministry has never been easy. We wish everything would go "by the book," but we know that is just not the reality. Maybe your beloved P.K. is presently going through a rough time spiritually and distancing himself from the Lord. Or perhaps he is now choosing to walk totally away from the Lord. Whatever the case, I'm sure his state of mind and choices are agonizing for you.

Please know that even the best of parents and ministers have had children who have "gone south spiritually." I believe it is possible to do everything right as a parent and yet, given their free will, your children may still choose to do "everything wrong" for a season.

Billy Graham's son Franklin had a period of time in his life when he chose not to follow the Lord. What a miracle of God's grace Franklin's testimony is now, as he follows so powerfully in his father's footsteps.

Oral Roberts' son, Richard, turned so far away from the Lord that he caused his parents many sleepless nights. Yet years later,

Richard has not only returned to the Lord, but is now the president of Oral Roberts University.

I'm reminded of the priceless Scripture that says, "Train up a child in the way he should go, and when he is old he will not depart from it (Proverbs 22:6)."[81] There may be periods of time that your children may not be serving the Lord, but the Word of God and the love that you have placed inside of them "will not return void."

Admittedly, it will be a time of great testing while you are waiting, praying, and working for things to truly turn around. It is always so much easier to be faith-filled and objective with other people's children. But when it is with your own children, the faith challenge usually feels much greater because your love is much greater. Just rest in the anchoring promise of Proverbs 22:6 given to all parents who have faithfully trained up their children "in the ways of the Lord." This chapter does not promise that your children will not have some spiritually rough times. Neither does it promise that your children will never spiritually walk away. But it *does* promise that they will not ultimately depart from it.

Dear Pastor, as a P.K., if I could tell you one thing...

Please don't think you're a bad parent if your child isn't serving God. We all make mistakes; and despite imperfections you may feel as a parent, the Word of God promises us that your investment of His Word in us will never return void.

- Lesley (Piersall) Butcher P.K.[82]

Just as the prodigal son returned to his father in Jesus' parable, so you can rest assured that as you remain faithful, God will bring your most beloved prodigal back to Himself should he or she ever choose to walk away. And because we understand that the pain is great for you as a parent, here are some suggestions for you from P.K.'s who've gone through these spiritually rocky times.

Steps to Bringing Them Around Spiritually:
Step 1 - Fight to keep the communication lines open.

Do whatever is necessary to keep the communication lines open with your struggling P.K.

In the final analysis, if you can keep your son or daughter talking to you, most everything will eventually work out. In short, there is no time period when communication is more imperative than when things start to unwind spiritually.

Perhaps one of a parent's greatest tools at this point is to find something that their P.K. is interested in and then use this area as a communication platform. During times of spiritual struggle, they may shut down, unwilling to communicate on spiritual issues. But wise parents very strategically focus on any conversation topic that might be of interest to their children without causing them to "shut down."

A parent of a rebellious P.K. shared recently about his new-found interest in wrestling. When I questioned his new, impassioned interest, his answer was very simple: "My son is shutting down on his mom and me. Things are going downhill pretty fast spiritually. About the only thing he'll still talk with us about is wrestling. So I'm cultivating my interest in wrestling because it's my only open door with my son. Let me tell you, if he wanted to talk about Chinese water polo, I'd be into that!" That is a wise parent talking.

Pause the "Preach," and listen patiently.

When the time seems right, ask sensitive, non-pushy, non-judg-mental questions about why they seem to be backing away spiritu-ally. Your P.K. will give you honest, insightful answers if they sense that you will listen without becoming pushy, defensive, or harsh. A great question to ask during these times would be something like, "What are the turnoffs to this whole God thing for you right now? Tell me what you're feeling and I promise I won't preach. I just want to really hear what you're feeling." Questions like this will help you discover when, how, and why their relationship with the Lord began to unravel. You should not ask these questions so that you can concoct the perfect answers or remedies, but so you can most importantly keep the lines of communication open and know how to specifically call out for your child in your private times of prayer.

Dear Pastor, as a P.K., if I could tell you one thing...

Communication is so important, telling your kids you love them, trust them, and showing them God's love without pressuring them. Communication that is open but without pressure, that's the big deal. - Anonymous P.K.

Above all, after you ask the questions, listen. Then after you've listened, listen some more. As a minister, it is likely that your immediate reaction is to kick into a communication mode that is very comfortable for you: preaching. With all the good intentions of a caring parent, it is easy to listen briefly and then begin to share with your P.K. a three-point-sermon on how to fix it. Stop! This kind of "sermonizing" is one of the main reasons that so many P.K.'s stated when asked why they grew to resent the ministry so deeply. It is precisely during those "heart-sharing times" that your P.K. does not want a preacher. Instead, they deeply want a caring, *listening* parent. There is a world of difference between the two.

During these times, your P.K. also doesn't want to feel like another one of your counseling "projects." Your child wants "deep listening" far more than "deep answering." Lee and Balswick further address this subject in a book about raising children in the ministry entitled *Life In a Glass House.* "It is ironic that many a clergyman, long trained in the area of social psychology, still handles family relationships as the pulpiteer. Even though he knows full well that behavior is more effectively altered by relationships that include love and encouragement, he may continue to preach at and preach about his own offspring. He is too likely to get at his own children by means of stern lectures, lengthy precepts, and finger-shaking commands. What Queen Victoria said of Gladstone might well be echoed by many a child of the parsonage: 'He insists upon addressing me as if I am a public audience.'"[83]

Dear Pastor, as a P.K., if I could tell you one thing...
You cannot force your kids to be super spiritual. Teach them when they are young and then allow them to apply God's will to their lives. Pressure will only turn them off. And one more thing, if you want them to listen to you, you need to first get really good at listening to them. - Anonymous P.K.

Ask caring questions that lead you to hear what your P.K.'s root offenses are and just continue to listen. They may say something like, "It feels like everyone expects too much of me, even you and Mom." Or you might hear something else like, "I'm sick of living life in a big fishbowl where everyone sees everything we do and tries to run my life." The key is not to *fix* it until you *feel* it. That's especially wise counsel when it comes to P.K.'s.

Step 2 - Guard against becoming overly emotional or reactionary.

Dear Pastor, as a P.K., if I could tell you one thing...
Hear your kids out, and learn to ask the right questions. Don't just get upset and get all fired up when they try to talk to you.
- Seth Macintosh, P.K[84].

When your child does begin to talk to you, avoid becoming emotional and reactionary. Obviously, if you allow emotions to emerge or reactions to control the discussion, the discussion will quickly end, as will your communication for quite awhile.

Differences between the communication style of a mom and dad often emerge during these challenging times. I am not saying that all parents (by their respective gender) react this way, but I have seen these differences in styles when addressing the kids. Moms tend to become more emotional and can escalate the situation through their highly charged responses that deepen the crisis. Dads tend to be more analytical and bottom-line in their approach. They size up the situation rather quickly, determine what they deem to be a suitable answer, and then make that answer known. In their minds, the answer to the entire situation appears a relatively easy one if the P.K. would merely "do what they need to do." If these responses sound familiar, then you may have to retrain yourself to respond better.

If you can avoid either one of these extremes, communication lines will continue to stay open and your children will feel comfortable expressing what is truly going on in their life. As you may already know, sometimes your P.K. says something just to see how you will react. Respond correctly by not reacting at all, and you'll hear what's really going on.

And that is the important thing to remember: to respond, not to react. By responding, you are rationally and thoughtfully providing what is best for your children. If you continue to do this, they will grow to listen to your responses. Oftentimes daughters especially are afraid of what their parents will say in specific circumstances, but if they have grown to trust that you will respond and not react, they'll be less apprehensive in communicating the good things as well as the bad.

Step 3 - Choose your battles wisely.

One area that I believe is significant in helping your P.K.'s come back to Christ is choosing your battles wisely. Too many battlegrounds arise when you address every aspect of their lives. This can cause you to lose the credibility to speak to them when it's really crucial. I'm not talking about letting things go, but I am talking about knowing which battles to fight.

If you are not careful about this, you may win the little battles but lose the war of bringing them back to Christ. Countless wars that often changed the course of history seemed to be victoriously won, but with a closer look there were a few battles lost along the way. The war's outcome oftentimes was won because of the strategy in choosing which battles to forfeit in order to win the war. The old phrase, "Don't strain at gnats and swallow camels," takes on its real meaning here.

I can think of one occasion that illustrates this quite well. A well-meaning pastor was rebuking his son for saying something that he didn't feel was theologically "agreeable" with him. The young P.K. wasn't swearing, using the Lord's name in vain or saying anything else crude of that nature, but the dad didn't agree with the phrase that his son used. I can understand a father wanting to give guidance, but he continued to push the issue instead of saying it once and then letting it drop. He majored on something that was relatively minor. After getting lectured to the full, the son yelled, "I haven't done drugs and I've never slept with anyone. I have never walked away from the Lord, and you're now majoring on this! Why don't we focus on what I haven't done instead of this small dumb issue? If you want me to, I could go out right now and give you something to really get mad at me about!"

Dear Pastor, as a P.K., if I could tell you one thing...
It has to be your child's decision to come back; just continue to show them love and not condemnation. - C.J. Smith[85]

Again, you have to ask yourselves if this battle is worth dying over. If it's not, value your battles enough to choose what holds the greatest significance. Learn to recognize why certain battles are upsetting you. Many times because of the position you are in it is easy to be upset because it endangers your reputation. It is humbling, but you must objectively decide that your biggest concern is the well being of your child, not your reputation. Choose to go easy on some of the less serious battles so that you can endure and win the war. Many times they want to see if it is your motivation to spare your reputation or them instead. They need to know they are most important.

Step 4 - Build on islands of strength.

Strengthening your relationship with your children to the point of seeing them make positive changes can be accomplished as you build on what I call "islands of strength." These are areas that they already enjoy and can easily become common ground. Islands of strength are just activities that they enjoy doing. It could be a sport or video game for a son and could be shopping for a daughter. If you join with them in these activities you will then have an island of strength to build upon.

I would like to point out that this "island of strength" can only be something that they really enjoy, but that might mean that this area could be something that you really don't enjoy. Lovingly said, deal with it. You may not even be very interested in it. Find out what's important to them and build on it. Talk to them about what they like to talk about. It's ideal if you both like the "island," but even if your son is a bowling fanatic and you can't stand the smell of those ugly shoes, become a bowling fanatic.

Learn to love what they love, and they'll love you for it!

My brothers and I tried nearly all sports, but baseball and softball became our favorites. Later I found out that he'd [my dad] secretly hoped we'd play basketball like he did, but I never knew that as he encouraged us and supported us both at practice and the games.

- Caleb Piersall, P.K. [86]

Step 5 - Find an "inside" support for your child.

One parenting technique that is often overlooked is finding your child an "inside support." What I mean is finding someone your son or daughter already looks up to and admires who has a strong relationship with Christ, a sharp Christian teenager or youth pastor. Seek them out.

Without your son or daughter knowing, call the individual and explain how much your son or daughter looks up to and respects them. Ask them privately to invest in your son or daughter, allowing their influence to make an impact on his or her life. Just by saying something like, "It would mean the world to me if you would occasionally hang out with Josh because he thinks so highly of you. I know you could really make a significant impact on him where others couldn't."

Like I said earlier, this person could also be a youth pastor or leader whom they admire. Even if the youth pastor doesn't pastor at your church, be secure enough to call someone who's involved in a ministry other than your own, because of the positive impact they may have on your son or daughter. The heartache, he or she will save you, will be worth going out on a limb for.

Dear Pastor, as a P.K., if I could tell you one thing...
You should know who your kids' friends are at all times. They rise and fall with their friends. - Jonathan French, P.K.[87]

As your son or daughter reflects on their budding relationship with this "inside support," continue to encourage the "inside" person about the impact he or she is making. Let them know that, "It really does make a huge difference when you take him/her out to spend time together." Then let those individuals know they are appreciated and supported. This arrangement will benefit them as well as your child. In being able to give to your child, they will find a sense of value and accountability.

This plan obviously works just as well for a son or daughter who is close to the Lord. I remember how my parents would ask specific people to invest time in my life. Three key people during my high school years spent large amounts of time taking care of me. Because I never "backslid" in my relationship with Christ, many youth pastors or leaders wouldn't have necessarily thought to hang out with me, just because they probably already thought of me as a "good kid."

I know my parents made encouraging comments to Melissa and Chad, two of the three people who reached out to me. My parents knew I loved these two and really looked up to them as friends and spiritual leaders. I know they never took care of me only because of a request from mom or dad, but I'm sure that the encouragement from my parents didn't hurt. I can say without hesitation that what Melissa and Chad invested into my life will never be taken for granted. [I love you guys, and Mercury will forever be a part of me! Thanks for becoming my "other" family!] Find the Melissa's and Chad's to place in your child's life, and you'll discover that the rewards will be overwhelming!

Step 6 - Do not provoke your children to wrath.

I'm sure that most of you will easily recall Ephesians 6:4, a verse that hits this point specifically. "And you, fathers, do not provoke your children to wrath, but bring them up in the training and admonition of the Lord."[88] I really don't need to spend much time on this suggestion, but please again remember a couple of key thoughts. Just as I had mentioned earlier, you can win the battle but lose the war by saying things that would provoke your kids to anger. You may be addressing the problem, but you are missing the point.

If you're trying to bring your children back into a strong relationship with Christ, they don't need to be corrected in every area that Christians are expected to measure up to. At this point in their life, they may not even be Christians. Your job is to allow the love of

Christ and His Spirit to draw them to Him by how you respond to them on a daily basis. Please major on the majors and minor on the minors. The Bible says it is the kindness of God that draws men to repentance. Allow yourself to love your kids back into the kingdom.

Lastly, when a discussion with opposing viewpoints arises which could potentially cause strife between you and your child, ask yourself one key question: "Do I always have to be right?" I'm sure that you as a parent in ministry are not this way, but there are numerous pastors that just cannot lose an argument. Yes, you may be right, but do you still always have to win? You're ultimately warring for your child's soul, not winning a minor battle about something that was done or said three days ago.

I think that many parents believe there is some "Secret Book to Being a Parent" that teaches that a parent always has to get in the last word. No! You are the mature one in the relationship - a role you must fill. When you are right, please give sound advice, but don't get in the last word just to get in the last word. When you do allow your child to have that coveted final word, don't make him or her pay for it by a bad attitude or a cold shoulder for the rest of the day. Yes, this does sound childish, but your son or daughter isn't the only one who occasionally will act like a child. It's when you personally don't allow yourself to be trapped in this battle that they are not provoked to wrath.

Yes, many times our children are the ones who begin the problem, but they need us, as parents, to take the higher, more mature road and stop it before it ever begins. When you take the high road with your children, you're not only stopping things that may provoke your P.K. to wrath, but you also are saving them from areas that could eventually bring about bitterness.

Again, choose your battles wisely.

One area that I believe is significant in helping your P.K.'s come back to Christ is choosing your battles wisely. Too many battlegrounds arise when you address every aspect of their lives. This can cause you to lose the credibility to speak to them when it's really crucial.

THINK ABOUT IT...

1. If one area significant in helping your P.K.'s come back to Christ is choosing your battles wisely, what are some battles you have been fighting lately? Are you focusing on the most important root issues that you are really concerned about? What can you change about your next conversation to help you focus on the overall picture of how your son or daughter is *really* doing emotionally and spiritually, instead of just trying to win a few minor battles?

2. One parenting technique that is often overlooked is finding your child an "inside support." Have you attempted to do this for your son or daughter? Who can you ask to be an "inside support" during this time?

3. The Bible says it is the kindness of God that draws men to repentance. Allow yourself to love your kids back into the kingdom. What areas of kindness do you know would begin to open up the heart of your child today?

Brian Dunn my adopted "big brother" who took Justin and I home every Sunday night for pizza after church so Mom and Dad could keep ministering.

Melissa (Dills) Neuman with me at my high school graduation (Melissa and Chad Bruegman were two of my small group leaders and an "inside support" for my parents - love you two)

CHAPTER 13

Avoiding The Traps Of Bitterness And Resentment

Most P.K.'s are bitter, I agree. I hate how people treated my mother. I really wanted to hurt people. I know that I am called, but I'm just not ready now. - Anonymous P.K.

Josh,

Hey, how's it going man? How's the ministry? Well, I'm just going to get straight to the point. Josh, this is my plea for help! From a P.K. to a P.K., help me out, man. My Dad was fired today by his church. Their reason was because he didn't have the right attitude in the office. My heart is so torn right now, dude. I don't know what to do. I want to just give up on my calling of being a youth pastor because of everything I've seen my Dad and my family go through. It's so hard to trust the ministry right now. I was all ready to graduate and head to Bible College, but now I don't know what to do.

I'm barely holding on to God. It's really hard to trust Him right now, you know. I know right now I can't even afford to go to Bible College. I mean, there goes my whole summer. My family worked harder at this church than at any church we've pastored, countless hours of blood and sweat, building everything, and countless hours on my knees praying for that church, only to get shafted.

Please tell your mom about this, too. I know she'll want to know about my parents and all. I love you, bro, and even though we don't know each other that well yet, I really feel like you're the only one that will give me a straight answer on this. Please pray your heart out for my family.

Love in Christ,
Anonymous P.K.

It bears repeating: raising your kids in the ministry is tough. Raising your kids at home without bitterness toward the ministry and God can at times be very difficult. Story after story could be told of pastor's kids who have become bitter and resentful of the ministry in which their parents serve. They begin to resent the painful moments that their family has endured. They gravitate to the hardening of their hearts and slowly become resentful as they hear comments about the ones they consider their heroes: their parents.

It's always amusing to me as I joke with other P.K.'s I meet, tongue in cheek, asking them, "So, did you have a rebellious period?" or "When did you last rebel?" (Remember, not all P.K.'s go through a rebellious phase—I didn't.)

I ask these questions because I realize that a definite connection exists between raising your kids in a home with forgiveness instead of justification and bitterness setting in against God and the ministry as they grew older. The connection is simple. If you strategically place guards that keep your kids from becoming bitter towards the ministry in your home, you will greatly decrease the likelihood of your kids needing "ministry" from influences outside of the home.

There are several "guards" that my parents have strategically placed within our home. These guards helped me look at individuals within the church as well-meaning people, not as "Satan's right hand of destruction." The decisions our parents made protected us from the issues that would have eventually created bitterness. Please know this: the guards that my parents established might be easy to list now, but they have been very difficult to follow.

Guard #1 - Avoid speaking about church disputes or problems in front of your children.

In my parent's Nebraska ministry, there was a Sunday school teacher that I admired greatly. Many times I would come home and say how amazing she was and how much I cared for her. While I was praising her, unbeknownst to me, she was about to receive what she called a "prophetic word" from God against my parents. She launched a pretty savage attempt to get them out of the church. While I would come to the dinner table and talk about how amazing the Sunday school teacher was, Dad and Mom repeatedly bit their lips and didn't say a word. They protected me.

Dear Pastor, as a P.K., if I could tell you one thing...

My parents protected me and hid things from me by not speaking negatively in front of me, and it worked. - Anonymous P.K.

If there is any one big area where I think pastors make the most mistakes, this is that area. I have one simple solution to this problem: don't talk about others... just don't. I would challenge anyone who believes that good comes from discussing church-related problems and disputes in front of their kids. What good can possibly come from this?

So many pastors today make this very common mistake. Sadly, the word "common" is very accurate; as I fear that many make this mistake because it's become a routine thing for so many to do. For those who had been previously raised in a "ministry" home, they may be used to this type of table talk, but having this background doesn't make it right.

"They never talked about things going on at church when they were home. If people were leaving the church or moving on, oftentimes we didn't even know about it. They never lied to us and always gave us the information we needed to know, so that when people asked us questions we weren't blind-sided."

- Ruth (Daugherty) Sanders, P.K.[89]

Guard #2 - When people hurt mom and dad, don't tell the kids.

One of the biggest issues P.K.'s deal with is seeing members of the congregation or ministry hurt their parents. One P.K. said, "As P.K.'s, we see the bad sides of people... the worst of humanity."

Although Guard #2 could be interlaced with Guard #1, it must be independently acknowledged. When people hurt you as parents, don't tell the kids. As I reflect on this "guard," I smile, thinking back to all the occasions that my parents lived out this rule. They really are pros. My father was especially careful in this area. I remember occasions where I would overhear him in a phone conversation at home or at the office. I would hear just enough to know that someone was causing a problem, a problem that wasn't benefiting my dad in any way. At that point, I would casually ask my dad what was going on. In typical Sam Mayo fashion, he would give me some vague answer that gave me no clue as to what was going on.

To this day, I may never know the details, but I know I was affected by seeing my parents hurt by so many Christian people.

- Kelli (Berteau) Williams, P.K.[90]

After a while, I knew under normal circumstances, there was no way my dad would ever tell me what had just happened in "those conversations." With time, though, I tried to get sneakier. I attempted to casually bring up the subject with an air of "I really don't care, but just tell me anyway." I even tried to bring up the incident later. At times I was relentless in trying to get my dad to say what was "eating him up" on the inside, but he wouldn't.

Dad never talked about the people in the church that were deeply hurting him, and he knew exactly what he was doing. He was protecting me from looking at people in a negative light, thus taking away the opportunity for me to grow bitter. My dad has always been protective of his home, and this silence was one way he protected us very well.

There is a story from Corrie Ten Boom's life in her book *The Hiding Place* that gives us an illustration of how to protect your son or daughter from carrying weights that they are not ready to bear. Corrie, whose family endured much hardship and loss during the Holocaust, tells the story as follows:

> "'Father, what is sex sin?'"
>
> My father turned to look at me, as he always did when answering a question, but to my surprise he said nothing. At last he stood up, lifted his traveling case from the rack over our heads, and set it on the floor.
>
> 'Will you carry it off the train, Corrie?' he said. I stood up and tugged at it. It was crammed with the watches and spare parts he had purchased that morning.
>
> 'It's too heavy,' I said.
>
> 'Yes,' he said. 'And it would be a pretty poor father who would ask his little girl to carry such a load. It's the same way, Corrie, with knowledge. Some knowledge is too heavy for children. When you are older and stronger, you can bear it. For now you must trust me to carry it for you.'
>
> And I was satisfied, more than satisfied, wonderfully at peace. There were answers to this and all my hard ques-

tions, but now I was content to leave them in my father's keeping."[91]

I have been satisfied to know that my parents were always protective of me by not "telling all," even though "telling all" might have been more satisfying to their "flesh" at the time.

Dear Pastor, as a P.K., if I could tell you one thing...
    Things will happen and circumstances will come that are not the ideal. When your kids are young and impressionable, do your best to shelter them. - Jonathan Piersall, P.K.[92]

Of course, there were moments when my brother and I did find out about incidences when my parents were hurt, and we did find out some of the "whos" and "whats." Those moments were very painful, but it was especially during those moments that my parents did everything they could to keep our hearts okay. They would either say something like "Hurt people...hurt people," or, "They meant well, but just went about it the wrong way." It's amazing what a simple one-liner can do when it is given by a trusted parent.

You can't shelter your kids from everything that could possibly make them bitter, but you can be wise and careful in your verbal responses during those times.

Guard #3 - Try to make everyone in your ministry circle look amazing to your kids.

I laugh thinking of all the times my parents lived out this point again and again. Many who know my parents may believe that this is a very natural characteristic for them, my mother especially. She may have an innate ability to encourage and lift others up, but our talks together all these years later have revealed how tough this was even for her at times.

There are many instances when your kids will see the good, the bad, and the ugly of ministry. Sadly, many times people within the church will appear more bad and ugly than good. Projects like building programs and other aspects of ministry that deal with money often become the catalyst to some of human nature's most negative characteristics.

I remember one such occasion when my parents had worked tirelessly to obtain a large sum of money for the church's building program, even sacrificing much out of our own personal finances. One member of the church had made a very large "faith promise" to the building fund. But several months later, at the height of financial pressure, this individual demanded a certain course of action from my parents. Feeling that this course of action was ethically questionable, they refused. Within days, the large financial commitment was revoked. Unbeknownst to me as a young boy, this angry church member was the father of a very close friend of mine.

At the height of the crisis, my friend and I were spending large amounts of time at each other's homes during the summer break. I'm sure it must have been very awkward for my parents, but they gave me absolutely no indication that anything was wrong. As a matter of fact, time after time, my parents spoke very affirming words about the family. They made every effort to reinforce only positive perceptions about these people in my mind. I smile as I recall that my brother and I later realized that our best indicator of a "problem person" in the church probably would have been our parents' heightened affirmations of them.

For those of us who have grown up in church, we know challenging events will happen, and turmoil is inevitable. But in the midst of this turmoil, it is your responsibility as parents not only to avoid the negative talk but also to emphasize the positive, create it when possible. Sometimes an awkward silence on your part will send a strong signal to your kids of your inner pain. Obviously, deception is not the goal. But my parents often tried to "crucify their flesh" by strategically saying kind things about people who were being every-thing but kind to them.

Dear Pastor, as a P.K., if I could tell you one thing...

Always make time for your kids and never let them hear the bad things. It's already hard enough. – Anonomous PK

Guard #4 - Don't give your kids the "leftovers."

My mom often talks about how at the end of the day she would drive her car into the garage, wearily grab her purse to walk inside, and mentally give herself the same one-line pep talk. "Jeanne, refuse to give your children the emotional leftovers." Night after night, my mother spent hours playing games, talking, and showing us that we were her number one priority. While other parents would choose to zone out by turning on the television, she would regularly give her family emotional energy that she probably didn't have.

One of the most significant traumas blasted into my parents' lives around my ninth birthday. As I previously mentioned, birthdays in the Mayo home are major events. That year was no exception. My mother enthusiastically hosted approximately thirty nine-year-old boys that afternoon, and never in my wildest dreams did I realize that the weight of the world was on her shoulders. She threw that party with such focused emotional attention that I remained completely unaware of the church storm that was brewing.

It has often been said that one of the truest measures of great-ness in a man or woman is how much it takes to deeply discourage them. If that is true, my parents mirrored true greatness on this occa-sion and countless others. Repeatedly, they just refused to give us easy reasons to resent the ministry or the Lord of the ministry. I am sure I'll never know the private price tags they paid in this process;

but I'm confident that those price tags have a great deal to do with the way Justin and I now perceive Christ's kingdom.

Dear Pastor, as a P.K., if I could tell you one thing...
When you're home, be home and never compromise the significance of family time for other concerns. - Christie Berteau, P.K.[93]

Guard #5 - Don't overprotect.

When we talk about overprotecting your kids, there is a movie that comes to my mind. The movie was called "Bubble Boy,"[94] and the plot surrounds a boy who grows up in a bubble. As the story unfolds, we learn that "Bubble Boy" has severe allergies that would kill him if he were ever to venture outside the plastic bubble that his doctor had placed him in. As "Bubble Boy" continued to grow into a young adult, his ever-increasing overprotective mother kept him from breaking out of this bubble into his desired freedom.

The end of the movie revealed quite a surprise. (I apologize because I'm about to ruin the ending of the movie for those of you who haven't seen it.) We learn that "Bubble Boy" actually grew out of his allergies at the early age of three. His overprotective mother never told her son the truth about the allergies because she wanted to "protect" him. Ironically, the mother was categorized as a "Christian" who didn't want her son to be "contaminated by the sins of the world."

This mother went to great lengths to protect her son from the evil influences that surrounded him. Near the conclusion of the movie, in a desire to chase after his lost love and find freedom, "Bubble Boy" escapes from his protective bubble. Although I can't say I recommend the movie, the point I'm trying to communicate is very apparent. Proper balance must be achieved in protecting your kids or you will merely "chase them away."

I strongly believe that a good parent in ministry can create a healthy balance between protecting their kids and not being overprotective. I don't claim that this task will be easy, but I am confident that it is prayerfully possible. Other ministerial leaders also share this view.

In Richard Willowby's article entitled "Prodigal Pk's,"[95] he states, "Ministers are exposed to so many hardships caused by sin and mistakes. We don't want our kids to be exposed to them." Sharon Collins, a minister's wife, says, "Being overprotective may actually push them toward greater rebellion and make them more vulnerable by keeping them more naive." Protect your kids, but don't become overbearing. It's the old quote that states, "Hold too tightly and you will find yourself holding nothing at all." I'm sure this is especially tough on ministers, because they have repeatedly seen up-close the high cost of wrong choices as they have ministered to numerous people outside of their family. But I distinctly remember my parents "loosening up" some of their protective guards as I got older. They realized the necessity of my learning how to build and value some safeguards of my own choosing.

Dear Pastor, as a P.K., if I could tell you one thing...

Try not to shelter your kids and protect them too much. It will only push them away and make them resent you in the process.

- Anonymous P.K.

Confirming Results from an Ontario P.K. Survey[96]

Not too long ago there was a study done on adult P.K.'s. Hundreds of surveys were sent back to the Ontario publication that conducted the survey. In this survey, one piece of data really grabbed my attention. They asked adult P.K.'s for suggestions on how to change the upbringing of P.K.'s. When I received this information, I was pleased to see that many of the things they suggested were the very same things I had written in this book. Even though several areas have already been mentioned, I felt the results would interest you. Some of the suggestions for ways to change the upbringing of P.K.'s were as follows:

- Be open and honest with your children
- Draw clear lines of communication
- Make your children feel deeply valued
- Let your children be themselves
- Keep your expectations reasonable; do not force them to volunteer or conform
- Allow your children to express their feelings
- Allow children to pursue their own beliefs
- Less prayer, Bible reading, church going
- Allow your kids to be active in community/outside church
- Always put your family first
- Make time for your children
- Eat together as a family and plan family events together
- Consume less alcohol

As I look over the list of suggestions that the over 400 adult Pk's gave, there are several ideas that stuck out to me. The points seemed to highlight valuing time with your children and not overexerting them in church activities. This again confirms to us that family has to be placed at the top of our priorities list.

I also found it very interesting that the suggestion of less alcohol was even mentioned. Being from a family that was always under the persuasion that alcohol has no place in the home, I found the fact that P.K.'s would recommend this for their families was not only humorous, but also eye-opening.

THINK ABOUT IT...

1. When you think about the most recent church disputes, or people who have hurt you lately, consider how you have allowed this to

be discussed at home. Are you proud of how you have handled yourself in front of your children? How can you improve your environment at home so that the "ups and downs" of ministry do not take a toll on the heart of your child?

2. When it comes to the time you spend with your children, do you ever feel like they are getting your emotional leftovers? How can you find a way to leave the hurt, the burdens, and the responsibilities of ministry at work so that when you come home you're "all there?"

3. Being overly protective can produce the opposite of what you originally intended by guarding your son or daughter. In what areas can you begin to loosen the reigns with your child? As you begin to let go you will see your child start to choose their own convictions and boundaries. How will this make you feel? How do you think this will make them feel? How will you respond to them if they disappoint you in their new freedom? How will you respond to them if they make some good choices?

**No emotional left-overs here...Dad is teaching
me how to shoot a basketball after coming home
from a long day at work**

A fun birthday party despite a difficult and busy season

CHAPTER 14

It All Boils Down To One Thing...

Teach us to number our days aright, that we may gain a heart of wisdom. - Psalm 90:12. [97]

A favorite story I like to recount teaches one lesson I pray you don't forget. It all really comes back to one thing — making time for what you love. The story goes like this:

1,000 Marbles

The older I get the more I enjoy Saturday mornings; perhaps it's the quiet solitude that comes with being the first to rise or just the unbounded joy of not having to be at work; either way, the first few hours of Saturday morning are my favorite. A few weeks ago, I was shuffling along the basement floor with a steaming cup of coffee in one hand and the morning paper in the other. What began as a typical Saturday morning for me turned into one of those life-altering lessons that life seems to hand you from time to time as the good Lord wills. Let me tell you about it.

I had turned the dial up on my C.B. radio in order to listen to a Saturday morning swap net. Along the way, I came across an older sounding gentleman with a tremendous signal and one of those captivating golden voices. He was telling whomever he was talking to something about a thousand marbles. I was intrigued, so I stopped to listen to what he had to say.

"Well, Tom," he said, "It sure sounds like you're really busy with your job, and I am sure that they pay you really well, but it's really a shame, Tom. It's a shame that you've had to be so busy and be away from your family and your church so much. Hard to believe a young man like you would have to work sixty or seventy hours a week to make ends meet. Too bad you missed your daughter's piano recital."

The older gentleman with the golden voice continued, "Let me tell you something, Tom, something that's helped me keep a good perspective in life, on my own priorities, in my own time."

"You see," he said, "I sat down one day and I did a little arithmetic. The average person, Tom, will live about seventy-five years. Then I multiplied 75 years times 52 weeks in a year and I came up with 3900, which is the number of Saturdays that the average person is going to have in his entire life; oh sure, some more, some less, but about 3900. "

"Okay, now stick with me, Tom. I'm getting to the important part," he said. "It took me until I was about 55 years old to think about all this in great detail and by that time, I had lived over 2800 Saturdays. So I got to thinking one day. If I lived to be 75 years old, I had only about 1000 Saturdays left to enjoy and to use however the good Lord would be most pleased."

"So I went to a toy store and bought every single marble they had. I ended up having to visit three toy stores to round up one thousand marbles. I took them home and I put them inside a large, clear plastic container right here in my shack, next to my gear; and now every Saturday since then, I've taken out one marble and I've thrown it away. "

"I found, Tom, that by watching the marbles diminish in my glass jar, I focus more on what's really important in life. Somehow, there's nothing like watching the time that the good Lord's given you on earth run out to help you keep your priorities straight."

"Let me tell you one more thing, Tom, before I sign off and take my lovely wife out for breakfast this morning. This very morning, Tom, I took the very last marble out of my container. I figure if the good Lord up in heaven gives me until next Saturday, He's given me a little extra time to keep doing things that really matter with my life."

"Time. Time. Tom, I guess it's been one of the greatest gifts, next to His Son Jesus, that He's given to all of us."

"Well, it's been nice to meet you, Tom; hope your life slows down a little bit and that somehow amidst your busy job, you figure out a way to spend more time with your family, your God, and the things that really count. Hope to meet you somewhere else on this C.B. band someday. Signing off for now. "

You could have heard a pin drop on that a.m. band when that wise old man signed off. I had planned to work on the antenna that morning and then was going to meet with some of the other a.m. enthusiasts and work on the next club newsletter. Instead, I walked into the kitchen to hug my wife. "Taking you and the kids to breakfast," I told her.

"Well, what brought this on?" she said smilingly.

"Ahh," I said. "It's just been a long time since I've spent a Saturday together with you and the kids. Hey, can we stop at a toy store while we are out? I need to buy some marbles."[98]

I haven't purchased any marbles yet. However, I am beginning to create some traditions with my wife to make the most of our "family time," marbles or no marbles, and that's what it's all about.

Let's brag.

Growing up as a pastor's kid is the best life your son or daughter could ever be privileged to live. I am convinced that there could be no other life that I would enjoy more than the one with which the Lord has blessed me.

As I've said before, this book has been about raising your kids successfully while balancing a life of ministry, as told from my prospective as a kid who grew up in it. My goal was to give you some basic pragmatics on how that can be accomplished. But, with most of the effort going towards telling you what to do and how to go about doing it, I don't want to leave a sour taste in your mouth.

In the process of encouraging and equipping you to be a sensitive parent to the ones who are "under the microscope," I don't want to forget to remind you how wonderfully blessed they are. If you do your best to keep a balance between ministry and home, your kids will have the greatest life possible. Sure, a life of ministry has its difficulties, but I wouldn't trade those difficulties for the countless blessings the Lord has given me in return.

Raising your son or daughter in the ministry is one of the best things for them in more ways than just the spiritual ones! Early in the 20th century a study was done which found that pastors' kids ran some of the largest companies in the United States (and those leaders are not all backslidden P.K.'s, either!).[99] The percentage of P.K. success is higher than those who were raised by parents within other professions. The ministry is the prime training ground for achievers and natural-born leaders.

In a book entitled *P.K.'s*, Cameron Lee[100] cites study after study showing that P.K.'s were less likely to "have rejected religion or to have left the church, less likely to drink, smoke, or stay up all night than other college freshmen who were not P.K.'s. P.K.'s had higher grades, better study habits, and more financial support came from scholarships. They were more involved in extracurricular activities; and more likely to have participated in state or regional speech and debate contests; and they were more likely to be presidents of student organizations. The researchers also found that ministers' children aspired to higher degrees and careers that emphasized social responsibility."

It is also interesting to note that parents who pray together once a day have a staggeringly low divorce rate of only 1%. For those of you in the ministry who pray with your spouse daily, feel the wonderful assurance of knowing that divorce in the homes of ministers, compared to the outside world, is very unlikely.

We as ministry kids really do have it great. Yes, there are P.K. causalities due to the war zone that ministry sometimes is. But honestly, I couldn't have asked for a better life. Sure it's difficult to be watched from every angle, and it isn't easy to feel like we are sharing our parents with everyone else who seems to breathe on this planet. But I will tell you this: there is something very special about knowing that you are different, different in a good way, and about realizing there is a call on your parents' lives that not many are privileged to have. It is a heritage, a priceless legacy.

No person could ever attach words to the kind of pride that your sons and daughters feel when they see you leading others to Christ. Walking in your steps and knowing what you have to offer this world gives them more pride than most kids could even begin to brag about. I really am proud to be a pastor's kid!

By the way, did I mention anywhere in this book that I'm now in the ministry full time?

THINK ABOUT IT...

Galatians 6:9: And let us not grow weary while doing good, for in due season we shall reap a harvest if we do not lose heart. [101]

1 Chronicles 28:20: And David said to his son Solomon, "Be strong and of good courage, and do it; do not fear nor be dismayed, for the Lord God – my God – will be with you. He will not leave you nor forsake you, until you have finished all the work for the service of the house of the Lord.[102]

Deuteronomy 6:5-7: You shall love the Lord your God with all your heart, with all your soul, and with all your strength. And these words which I command you today shall be in your heart. You shall teach them diligently to your children, and shall talk of them when you sit in your house, when you walk by the way, when you lie down, and when you rise up.[103]

2 Thessalonians 3:5: Now may the Lord direct your hearts into the love of God and into the patience of Christ.[104]

2 Corinthians 4:1: Therefore, since we have this ministry, as we have received mercy, we do not lose heart.[105]

What a legacy of ministry – a picture of Grandpa Mayo's traveling ministry

Me with Grandpa Mayo

Dear Mom & dad,

well, Today was big day I actually felt anointed. I talked about familys. Thanks for making the talk so easy. You two have truly been the "god given" parents. No divorce, on struggle, no pain, I cant thank you two enough. You have brought me up to be a man of God and I am eternally greatful for giving me the choice of life. Lord, I owe you thanks for my parents. The largest present, besides you, that you could even give me. May You give me what you have given my parents. Thanks Mom. Dad thanks. You will know how much the answered questions and talks are worth to me. You two have set a standard from the Lord himself and I hope to follow "in his steps". Heaven know of all your sacrifices thanks

Love,
your first born

Letter to Mom and Dad

**Mom and I serving together in full-time ministry…
this is the first fall Youth retreat we ran together**

The Mayos

My wedding day – the beginning of my family

And just for fun…a picture of the ministry Monica and I are currently privileged to direct

Endnotes

[1] Lee, Cameron and Balswick, Jack. 1989. *Life in a Glass House: The Minister's Family in its Unique Social Context.* Grand Rapids, Michigan: Zondervan.

[2] Lester Sumrall, personal interview. 2002

[3] Matthew Swaggart, personal interview. 2002

[4] Lesley (Piersall) Butcher, Personal interview, 2002

[5] Wyon, Olive. <as quoted in> Bickel, Bruce and Jantz, Stan. 1999. God is in the Small Stuff for Your Family. Uhrichsville, Ohio: Promsie Press. pp. 154

[6] I Peter 1:7. Peterson, Eugene. The Message Bible. 2002. Navpress Publishing.

[7] Hebrews 4:15. New Living Translation. 1996 Tyndale Publishing.

[8] Luke 14:28. New Living Translation.1996 Tyndale Publishing.

[9] Vanessa Cobbs. Personal Response. Open-ended survey results, 2002.

[10] Marcus Haggard. personal interview 2002.

[11] Anonymous. Personal response. Open-ended survey results, 2002.

[12] "It takes a village…" African Proverb. . Farsi, S.S. *Swahili Sayings from Zanzibar*. Vol 1, Proverbs, 1958, Nairobi: East African Literature Bureau.

[13] "Parents are prone…" Emma K Hubburt. http://www.zona-pellucida.com/critical3.html. <As quoted in> Elmore, Tim. *Nurturing the Leader Within Your Child.* . 2001. Nashville, TN: Thomas Nelson Publishing. Pp. 128.

[14] Kelli (Berteau) Williams. Personal Interview 2002.

[15] Z.H. Personal response. Open-ended survey results 2002

[16] Psalms 90:12. New Living Translation. 1996 Tyndale Publishing.

[17] Independent Survey. Lesley (Piersall) Butcher. Results documented

[18] Hannah (Conneely-Hall). Personal Interview. 2002

[19] Jacob Epstein and George Bernard Shaw. Conversation. Braude, Jacob. 1971. *Speaker's and toastmaster's handbook of anecdotes by and about famous personalities.* Prentice-Hall Publishing. Pp. 52

[20] John Daugerty. Personal Response. Open-ended survey results 2002.

[21] Marcus Haggard. Personal Interview. 2002

[22] Matt Swaggart. Personal Interview. 2002

[23] Ruth (Duagherty) Sanders. Personal Interview. 2002

[24] Christie Berteau. Personal Interview. 2002

[25] Independent Survey. Lesley (Piersall) Butcher. Results documented

[26] Elmore, Tim. *Nurturing the Leader Within Your Child.* 2001. Nashville, TN: Thomas Nelson Publishing. Pp. 127

[27] Betterhein, Bruno. *A Good Enough Parent.* 1987. New York: Random House Publications. Pp. 14

[28] Hesburght, Theodor. "The most important thing a father can do for his children is love their mother." <http://www.wisdomquotes.com/001765.html> Copyright 1995-2006. Jone Johnson Lewis

[29] Jonathan Piersall. Personal Interview 2002

[30] John Mason. One good action is worth a thousand intentions.

[31] Song of Solomon 1:6. New Revised Standard Version. 2004 Hendrickson Publishing

[32] Joy Delgatty. Personal Response. Open-ended survey results. 2002

[33] Author Anonymous. Dr. Jim Denison. 2005. Adult Online Bible Commentary. Lesson Eleven. Baptist Press. Pp. 75

[34] Ruth (Daugherty) Sanders. Personal Interview. 2002

[35] Mary Queen of Scotland. I fear John Knox's prayers. . Progress of Nations, ed. Sylvester, Charles. 1912. Hanson-Bellows Company. Vol III, pp. 454-457.

[36] Independent survey. Lesley (Piersall) Butcher. Results documented.

[37] Tea Story, as told in, www. Sermonillustrations.com., "ordinary," <as quoted in> Morris Mandel in *Jewish Press* K. Hughes, <u>Liberating Ministry From The Success Syndrome</u>, Tyndale, 1988, p. 133.

[38] Kelli (Berteau) Williams. Personal Interview. 2002

[39] Jason McCutchen. Personal Response. Open-ended survey results. 2002.

[40] Tevye. Fiddler on the Roof. Original Broadway Production. 1964. RCA

[41] Marcus Haggard. Personal Interview. 2002

[42] RJ Tate. Personal Interview. 2002

[43] Emerson, Ralph Waldo "The years will teach you what the days will never know." *Essays, 2nd Series.* "Experience." 1844. pp. 483.

[44] Proverbs 13:20. New Living Translation. 1996. Tyndale Publishing.

[45] Daniel McIntosh. Personal Interview. 2002

[46] Psalms 61:5. Scripture taken from the New King James Version®. Copyright © 1982 by Thomas Nelson, Inc. Used by permission. All rights reserved.

[47] Independent survey. Lesley (Piersall) Butcher. Results documented.

[48] Proverbs 6:26. American Standard Version. 1901.

[49] "Precious" Hebrew Concordance. Kohlenberger III, John; Strong, James, & Swanson, James. *Strong Concordance.* 2001. Zondervan Publishing. Pp.

[50] Jim Elliot. Elliot, Elisabeth. *The Journals of Jim Elliot.* 1978. Grand Rapids, Michigan: Baker Book House Co. pp 174.

[51] Vanessa Cobbs. Personal Response. Open-ended survey results. 2002

[52] Native Story, as told in, www. Sermonillustrations.com., "prayer," <as quoted in> *Today in the Word*, June 29, 1992.

[53] Jonathan French. Personal Interview. 2002

[54] Independent Survey. Lesley (Piersall) Butcher. Results documented

[55] Jarod Cooper Story, http://www.paradigm-mag.co.uk/archive.html

[56] Lee, Cameron and Balswick, Jack. 1989. *Life in a Glass House: The Minister's Family in its Unique Social Context.* Grand Rapids, Michigan: Zondervan. Pp. 172.

[57] Roshenhan, David. Psychological Experiment. Rosenhan, D. (1973) On being sane in insane places. *Science* 179, pp. 250-258.

[58] Lee, Cameron and Balswick, Jack. 1989. *Life in a Glass House: The Minister's Family in its Unique Social Context.* Grand Rapids, Michigan: Zondervan. Pp. 169.

[59] Heather Wheeler. Personal Response. Open-ended survey results. 2002.

[60] Joy Delgatty. Personal Response. Open-ended survey results. 2002.

[61] Tom Barker. Personal Response. Open-ended survey results..2002

[62] Stephen Piersall. Personal Interview. 2002

[63] RJ Tate. Personal Interview. 2002

[64] Rachelle (Sumrall) Pagewood. Personal Interview. 2002

[65] Ashleigh Hancock. Personal Response. Open-ended survey results.

[66] Jason McCutchen. Personal Response. Open-ended survey results.

[67] Sharon Collins, MD. Cedar Rapids, Iowa. as quoted in: Willoby, Richard. "Prodigal PK's" *Pastor's Family Magazine.* October/November, 1996. Focus on the Family.

[68] Heather Wheeler. Personal Response. Open-ended survey results

[69] Caleb Piersall. Personal Interview. 2002

[70] Richard Willoby. *Prodigal PK's. Pastor's Family Magazine.* October/November, 1996. Focus on the Family.

[71] Aaron Hellfinstine. <personal response / discovered quote?>

[72] Leadership Magazine. Survey Results. "Is the Pastor's Family Safe at Home?" *Leadership*. Fall 1992, pp. 38-44.

[73] Seth Mcintosh. Personal Interview. 2002

[74] Lesley (Piersall) Butcher. Personal Interview. 2002

[75] Romans 8:28. New Living Translation. 1996 Tyndale Publshing

[76] "Trust His Heart." Eddie Carswell & Babbie Mason copyright ©1989 Word Music, Inc.

[77] Ruth (Daugherty) Sanders. Personal Interview. 2002

[78] Nathan Piersall. Personal Interview. 2002

[79] Sarah (Daugherty) Wehrli .Personal response. Open-ended survey results

[80] Justin Mayo. Personal Interview. 2002

[81] Proverbs 22:6. Scripture taken from the New King James Version®. Copyright © 1982 by Thomas Nelson, Inc. Used by permission. All rights reserved.

[82] Lesley (Piersall) Butcher. Personal Interview. 2002

[83] As quoted in: Wynn, JC. "Consider the Children," *Pastoral Psychology.* 11 (September, 1960). Pp. 23.

[84] Seth McIntosh. Personal Interview. 2002

[85] CJ Smith. Personal Interview. 2002

[86] Caleb Piersall. Personal Interview. 2002

[87] Jonathan French. Personal Interview. 2002

[88] Ephesians 6:4. New King James Version. 1982 Thomas Nelson Publishing.

[89] Ruth (Daugherty) Sanders. Personal Interview. 2002

[90] Kelli (Berteau) Williams. Personal Interview. 2002

[91] *The Hiding Place* by Corrie tenBoom with John and Elizabeth Sherrill. 1971. Chosen Books LLC, Chappaqua, New York

[92] Jonathan Piersall. Personal Interview. 2002

[93] Christie Berteau, Personal interview. 2002

[94] Bubble Boy. 2001. WGA. Written by: Cinco Paul & Ken Daurio.

[95] Willoby, Richard. "Prodigal PK's." *Pastor's Family Magazine.* October/ November, 1996. Focus on the Family.

[96] Survey. Cambell, DouglasThe Clergy Family in Canada: Focus on Adult Pk's. Erindale College, University of Toronto.

[97] Scripture taken from the Holy Bible, New International Version®. Copyright © 1973, 1978, 1984 by International Bible Society. Used by permission of Zondervan Publishing House. All rights reserved.

[98] 100 marbles story. Orignially quoted from Jeanne Mayo, NYLC, 2002, Story also found in: *Nurturing the Leader Within Your Child.* 2001. Nashville: Thomas Nelson Publishing. Pp 142-143.

[99] 20th Century PK study. <As quoted in> Farrel, Bill & Pam. "Relationships! Help your kids by loving!" *San Diego County's Christian Newspaper.* http:// www.goodnewsetc.com/2FAM71.htm

[100] Lee, Cameron. *PK: Helping Pastor's Kids through Their Identity Crisis.* 1992. Zondervan Publishing.

[101] Galatians 6:9. Scripture taken from the New King James Version®. Copyright © 1982 by Thomas Nelson, Inc. Used by permission. All rights reserved.

[102] I Chronicles 28:20. Scripture taken from the New King James Version®. Copyright © 1982 by Thomas Nelson, Inc. Used by permission. All rights reserved.

[103] Deuteronomy 6:5-7. Scripture taken from the New King James Version®. Copyright © 1982 by Thomas Nelson, Inc. Used by permission. All rights reserved.

[104] II Thessalonians 3:5. Scripture taken from the New King James Version®. Copyright © 1982 by Thomas Nelson, Inc. Used by permission. All rights reserved.

[105] II Corinthians 4:1. Scripture taken from the New King James Version®. Copyright © 1982 by Thomas Nelson, Inc. Used by permission. All rights reserved.

CPSIA information can be obtained at www.ICGtesting.com
Printed in the USA

243240LV00014B/101/A